First World War
and Army of Occupation
War Diary
France, Belgium and Germany

37 DIVISION
63 Infantry Brigade
Lincolnshire Regiment
8th Battalion
1 March 1916 - 31 March 1919

WO95/2529/1

The Naval & Military Press Ltd
www.nmarchive.com
Published in association with The National Archives

Published by

The Naval & Military Press Ltd

Unit 10 Ridgewood Industrial Park,

Uckfield, East Sussex,

TN22 5QE England

Tel: +44 (0) 1825 749494

www.naval-military-press.com

www.nmarchive.com

This diary has been reprinted in facsimile from the original. Any imperfections are inevitably reproduced and the quality may fall short of modern type and cartographic standards.

© Crown Copyright
Images reproduced by permission of The National Archives, London, England, 2015.

Contents

Document type	Place/Title	Date From	Date To
Heading	WO95/2529/1		
Heading	Reference WO95/2529 8th Bn Lincoln Regt. Aug 1916-Mar 1919		
Heading	37th Division 63rd Infy Bde 8th Bn Lincoln Regt. Aug 1916-Mar 1919. From 21 Div		
War Diary	Trenches	01/08/1916	05/08/1916
War Diary	Camblain L'Abbe	06/08/1916	12/08/1916
War Diary	Dieval	13/08/1916	23/08/1916
War Diary	Villers-Au. Bois.	24/08/1916	02/09/1916
War Diary	Fresnicourt	03/09/1916	17/09/1916
War Diary	Sain.	18/09/1916	30/09/1916
Miscellaneous			
Miscellaneous	A Form. Messages And Signals		
War Diary	Trenches Souchey II	01/10/1916	13/10/1916
War Diary	Trenches Souchey I	14/10/1916	16/10/1916
War Diary	Coupigny	17/10/1916	17/10/1916
War Diary	Frevilliers	18/10/1916	19/10/1916
War Diary	Denier	20/10/1916	20/10/1916
War Diary	Emplier	21/10/1916	21/10/1916
War Diary	Raincheval	22/10/1916	29/10/1916
War Diary	Beauval	30/10/1916	07/11/1916
War Diary	Lucheux	08/11/1916	11/11/1916
War Diary	Acheux	12/11/1916	14/11/1916
War Diary	Trenches	14/11/1916	26/11/1916
War Diary	Mailly Maillet.	27/11/1916	30/11/1916
War Diary	Sarton.	01/12/1916	13/12/1916
War Diary	Mezerolles.	14/12/1916	14/12/1916
War Diary	Conchy	15/12/1916	15/12/1916
War Diary	Huclier	16/12/1916	16/12/1916
War Diary	Amettes	17/12/1916	17/12/1916
War Diary	La Pierriere	18/12/1916	21/12/1916
War Diary	Lestrum	22/12/1916	31/12/1916
War Diary	Vieille Chapelle	31/12/1916	01/01/1917
War Diary	Fosse	02/01/1917	07/01/1917
War Diary	Trenches	08/01/1917	15/01/1917
War Diary	Locon Area	16/01/1917	27/01/1917
War Diary	Trenches	28/01/1917	31/01/1917
Miscellaneous	To 37 Div Q.	28/02/1917	28/02/1917
War Diary	Trenches	01/02/1917	01/02/1917
War Diary	Bethune	02/02/1917	11/02/1917
War Diary	Mazingarbe	12/02/1917	13/02/1917
War Diary	Trenches	14/02/1917	24/02/1917
War Diary	Mazingarbe	25/02/1917	28/02/1917
War Diary	Mazingarbe	01/03/1916	01/03/1916
War Diary	Bethune.	02/03/1916	02/03/1916
War Diary	Robecq	03/03/1916	03/03/1916
War Diary	Boerecq	04/03/1916	08/03/1916
War Diary	Tangry	09/03/1917	09/03/1917
War Diary	Neuville Au Cornet	10/03/1917	31/03/1917
Miscellaneous	To 37 Div Q.	01/05/1917	01/05/1917

War Diary	Neuville Au Cornet	01/04/1917	03/04/1917
War Diary	Givenchy	05/04/1917	05/04/1917
War Diary	Lattre St Quentin.	07/04/1917	07/04/1917
War Diary	Duisans.	08/04/1917	08/04/1917
War Diary	Arras	09/04/1917	12/04/1917
War Diary	Duisans	13/04/1917	13/04/1917
War Diary	Beaufort.	14/04/1917	20/04/1917
War Diary	Arras	23/04/1917	29/04/1917
War Diary	Beaufort	30/04/1917	30/04/1917
Miscellaneous	8th Battalion, The Lincolnshire Regiment. Appendix 1	16/04/1917	16/04/1917
Heading	War Diary 8th Lincolnshire Regt May. 1917. Vol.20		
War Diary	Beaufort.	01/05/1917	21/05/1917
War Diary	Arras	22/05/1917	31/05/1917
Heading	War Diary 8th Lincolns June 1917. Vol.21		
Miscellaneous	Form. Messages And Signals		
War Diary	Beaufort	01/06/1917	04/06/1917
War Diary	Croisette	05/06/1917	05/06/1917
War Diary	Heuchin	06/06/1917	06/06/1917
War Diary	Fruges.	07/06/1917	08/06/1917
War Diary	Radinghem.	09/06/1917	21/06/1917
War Diary	Rely	22/06/1917	22/06/1917
War Diary	Steenbecque	23/06/1917	23/06/1917
War Diary	Caestre.	24/06/1917	24/06/1917
War Diary	Brulooze.	25/06/1917	28/06/1917
War Diary	Trenches.	29/06/1917	30/06/1917
Heading	War Diary 8th Lincolns July 1917. Vol.22		
Miscellaneous	A Form. Messages And Signals.		
War Diary	Trenches.	01/07/1917	01/07/1917
War Diary	Mt Kemmel.	02/07/1917	09/07/1917
War Diary	Trenches	10/07/1917	19/07/1917
War Diary	Kemmel Hill.	20/07/1917	24/07/1917
War Diary	Trenches.	25/07/1917	26/07/1917
War Diary	Kemmel Hill.	27/07/1917	28/07/1917
War Diary	Trenches.	29/07/1917	31/07/1917
Heading	War Diary 8th Lincolns Aug. 1917. Vol.23		
Miscellaneous	A Form. Messages And Signals.		
War Diary	Trenches.	01/08/1917	01/08/1917
War Diary	Bailleul	02/08/1917	07/08/1917
War Diary	Chinese Wall.	08/08/1917	14/08/1917
War Diary	Trenches.	15/08/1917	21/08/1917
War Diary	Chinese Wall	22/08/1917	25/08/1917
War Diary	Westoutre.	26/08/1917	28/08/1917
War Diary	Bois Confluent.	29/08/1917	31/08/1917
Heading	War Diary 8th Lincolns Sept 1917. Vol.24		
War Diary	Bois Confluent.	01/09/1917	01/09/1917
War Diary	Trenches	02/09/1917	06/09/1917
War Diary	Rossignol Wood.	07/09/1917	09/09/1917
War Diary	Berthen.	10/09/1917	18/09/1917
War Diary	Kemmel	19/09/1917	20/09/1917
War Diary	Mt. Kokereele.	21/09/1917	26/09/1917
War Diary	Shrewsbury Forest	27/09/1917	30/09/1917
Heading	War Diary 8th Lincoln Regt. Oct 1917. Vol.25		
Miscellaneous	63rd Infantry Brigade.	01/11/1917	01/11/1917
War Diary	Trenches.	01/10/1917	05/10/1917
War Diary	In Trenches.	06/10/1917	06/10/1917
War Diary	Kemmel	07/10/1917	09/10/1917

War Diary	Trenches.		10/10/1917	20/10/1917
War Diary	Near Merris.		21/10/1917	22/10/1917
War Diary	Merris.		23/10/1917	31/10/1917
Miscellaneous	A Form. Messages And Signals.			
War Diary	Merris.		01/11/1917	08/11/1917
War Diary	Dranoutre.		09/11/1917	09/11/1917
War Diary	Bois Carre.		10/11/1917	16/11/1917
War Diary	La Clytte.		17/11/1917	24/11/1917
War Diary	Trenches.		25/11/1917	04/12/1917
War Diary	Spoil Bank		05/12/1917	12/12/1917
War Diary	Murrumbidgee.		13/12/1917	20/12/1917
War Diary	Trenches.		21/12/1917	28/12/1917
War Diary	Tournai Camp.		29/12/1917	31/12/1917
Heading	63rd Brigade. 37th Division. 8th Battalion The Lincoln Regiment. January 1918			
War Diary	Tournai Camp.		01/01/1918	04/01/1918
War Diary	Murrumbidgee.		05/01/1918	10/01/1918
War Diary	Mic Mac Camp.		11/01/1918	20/01/1918
War Diary	Wallon Cappel.		21/01/1918	31/01/1918
Heading	63rd Brigade. 37th Division. 8th Battalion The Lincoln Regiment. February 1918			
War Diary	Wallon Cappel.		13/02/1918	13/02/1918
War Diary	Foresters Camp		14/02/1918	14/02/1918
War Diary	Trenches.		15/02/1918	20/02/1918
War Diary	Scottish Wood.		21/02/1918	22/02/1918
War Diary	Canada Tunnels.		23/02/1918	24/02/1918
War Diary	Trenches.		25/02/1918	28/02/1918
Heading	63rd Brigade. 37th Division. 8th Battalion The Lincoln Regiment. March 1918			
War Diary	Scottish Wood Camp.		01/03/1918	08/03/1918
War Diary	Trenches.		09/03/1918	15/03/1918
War Diary	Canada Tunnels.		16/03/1918	21/03/1918
War Diary	Scottish Wood Camp.		22/03/1918	24/03/1918
War Diary	Trenches.		25/03/1918	27/03/1918
War Diary	Billets.		28/03/1918	31/03/1918
Heading	63rd Brigade. 37th Division. 8th Battalion The Lincoln Regiment. April 1918			
War Diary	Henu Trenches.		01/04/1918	01/04/1918
War Diary	S.E. Of Gommecourt.		02/04/1918	06/04/1918
War Diary	Gommecourt Wood.		07/04/1918	09/04/1918
War Diary	S.E. Of Gommecourt.		09/04/1918	14/04/1918
War Diary	N. Of Gommecourt Wood Henu.		15/04/1918	15/04/1918
War Diary	Henu Authie.		16/04/1918	22/04/1918
War Diary	Trenches.		23/04/1918	30/04/1918
Heading	63rd Brigade. 37th Division. 8th Battalion The Lincoln Regiment. May 1918			
War Diary	Trenches.		01/05/1918	31/05/1918
Heading	63rd Brigade. 37th Division. 8th Battalion The Lincolnshire Regiment. June 1918			
War Diary	Trenches.		01/06/1918	30/06/1918
Heading	63rd Brigade. 37th Division. 8th Battalion The Lincolnshire Regiment. July 1918			
War Diary	Trenches.		01/07/1918	07/07/1918
War Diary	Souastre.		08/07/1918	09/07/1918
War Diary	Trenches.		10/07/1918	26/07/1918
War Diary	Souastre.		27/07/1918	29/07/1918

War Diary	Trenches.	30/07/1918	31/07/1918
Heading	63rd Brigade. 37th Division. 8th Battalion The Lincolnshire Regiment. August 1918		
War Diary	Trenches.	01/08/1918	31/08/1918
Heading	63rd Brigade. 37th Division. 8th Battalion The Lincolnshire Regiment. September 1918		
War Diary	Achiet. Le. Petit.	01/09/1918	02/09/1918
War Diary	Trenches.	03/09/1918	11/09/1918
War Diary	Lebucquiere.	12/09/1918	16/09/1918
War Diary	Trenches.	17/09/1918	22/09/1918
War Diary	Thilloy.	23/09/1918	30/09/1918
Heading	63rd Brigade. 37th Division. 8th Battalion The Lincolnshire Regiment. October 1918		
War Diary	Royaulcourt.	01/10/1918	07/10/1918
War Diary	Trenches.	08/10/1918	12/10/1918
War Diary	Caudry.	13/10/1918	22/10/1918
War Diary	Briastre.	23/10/1918	23/10/1918
War Diary	Beaurain Neuville.	24/10/1918	31/10/1918
Heading	63rd Brigade. 37th Division. 8th Battalion The Lincolnshire Regiment. November 1918		
War Diary		01/11/1918	04/11/1918
War Diary	Neuville.	05/11/1918	11/11/1918
War Diary	Caudry.	12/11/1918	30/11/1918
Heading	63rd Brigade. 37th Division. 8th Battalion The Lincolnshire Regiment. December 1918		
War Diary	Caudry.	01/12/1918	01/12/1918
War Diary	Montrecourt.	02/12/1918	02/12/1918
War Diary	Villers Pol.	03/12/1918	14/12/1918
War Diary	Bavai.	15/12/1918	15/12/1918
War Diary	Sous-Le-Bois.	16/12/1918	17/12/1918
War Diary	Grand-Reng.	18/12/1918	18/12/1918
War Diary	Binche.	19/12/1918	19/12/1918
War Diary	Courcelles.	20/12/1918	20/12/1918
War Diary	Frasnes-Lez-Gosselies.	21/12/1918	10/03/1919
War Diary	Jumet.	11/03/1919	31/03/1919

WO 95 2529/-

REFERENCE

WO
95

2529

8th BN LINCOLN
REGT.
AUG 1916 – MAR
1919

CONSERVATION DEPARTMENT

11-3-1999

37TH DIVISION
63RD INFY BDE

8TH BN LINCOLN REGT.
AUG 1916-MAR 1919.

From 21 Div 63BDE

WAR DIARY
or
INTELLIGENCE SUMMARY

Army Form C. 2118

Pages 16
Mar '19

8 Lincoln Regt
VOL II

Place	Date	Hour	Summary of Events and Information	Remarks and references to Appendices
TRENCHES	1-8-16		BN. in "BERTHONVAL" SECTOR. Casualties 2 men wounded. Lt. R.A. PRESTON left Bn. for R.F.C.	2 App R17
"	2-8-16		Bn. in trenches. Quiet day. Reinforcement of 1 officer. Lt. J. Wiggins.	28 App R17
"	3.8.16		BN in trenches. Enemy trench mortars rather active on left. Casualties 3 men wounded (2 severely wounded)	28 App R17
"	4.8.16		BN in trenches Casualties 2 rifle grenadiers wounded. 2 men previously reported severely wounded now reported "Died of Wounds"	28 App R17
"	5.8.16		Bn. in trenches. Bde. Op. O.72 received. A quiet day. Casualties nil.	28 App R17
"	6.8.16		Bn. relieved in the trenches by 10 Bn. York & Lancaster Regt. and billeted in CAMBLAIN L'ABBE.	28 App R17 28 App R17
CAMBLAIN L'ABBE	7.8.16		BN. in Billets. Bathing and refitting. 2/6 Lilly Road Bunker under instruction in Lewis gun. No 3 Co. prinig a Range. Bn found working party 2 off 100 NCO & men	28 App R17
"	8.8.16		Bn in Billets. Training carried on. 182nd Tun. Cy R.E.	28 App R17
"	9.8.16		Bn in Billets. Training carried on. 20 off 100 ⟨men⟩ " " " 1 off	28 App R17
"	10.8.16		Bn in Billets. Training carried on. D Coy on Range.	28 App R17
"	11.8.16		Bn in Billets. Training carried out. D Coy on Range.	28 App R17
"	12.8.16		Bn in Billets. NCOs men of the new draft (200) trained. 230 NCOs men attached to 176 Coy. R.E. for Fay. rations and waterline.	28 App R17
"	13.8.16		BN. moved & billeted in DIEVAL. arrived about 2 A.M.	28 App R17
DIEVAL	14.8.16		Bn in Billets. Inspection carried out — rifles, ammunition, bayonet.	28 App R17

WAR DIARY or INTELLIGENCE SUMMARY

Army Form C.2118

Place	Date	Hour	Summary of Events and Information	Remarks and references to Appendices
DIEVAL	15.8.16		Bn. in billets. Training carried out.	1/3 R.W.F.
"	16.8.16		Bn. in billets. Training carried out as per syllabus.	2/3 R.W.F.
"	17.8.16		Bn. in billets. Training carried out as per syllabus.	2/3 R.W.F.
"	18.8.16		Bn. in billets. " " "	2/3 R.W.F.
"	19.8.16		Bn. " " O/C attended Conference at 1V Corps H.Q.	O/C 2/3 R.W.F.
"	20.8.16		Bn. " " (Sunday)	2/3 R.W.F.
"	21.8.16		Bn. " " Training carried out.	2/3 R.W.F.
"	22.8.16		Bn. " " working party of 200 N.C.O.s and men. 4 officers at CUVIGNY FM.	2/3 R.W.F.
"	23.8.16		Bn. moved to VILLERS-AU-BOIS. Working party of 120 N.C.O.s and men + 3 officers at CUVIGNY FM. 2 offs 111 N.C.O.s and men attached to G.O.C. 2/1 R.W.F. (9th Div.)	2/3 R.W.F.
VILLERS-AU-BOIS	24.8.16		Bn. in billets (in emergency under orders of 9th Div.) 'A' Coy bombers throwing live bombs on range.	2/3 R.W.F.
"	25.8.16		Bn. in billets. Training carried out. 'C' firing on range. A. White from 9th & 3rd Bns. rejd. Bombers Bn. bathed at CAMBLAIN L'ABBÉ. 2/Lt. D.C. Hodgson Reinforcement of 3 officers.	R.W.F. 2/3 R.W.F.
"	26.8.16		Am. in billets. Training carried out. Bn. Transport Competition S/Sec. R. 1st Prize for best Pm. Parade. Times as G.S. wagon & Pair H.D. Horses. 1st Prize for limber out 2/3 R.W.F. of Mules. 2/3 R.W.F.	2/3 R.W.F.
"	27.8.16		Am. in billets. Training carried out. Inspection of Transport by O/C Divisional Train. 2/3 R.W.F.	
"	28.8.16		Bn. in billets. Training carried out. 2 officers and 111 N.C.O.s and men attached to	2/3 R.W.F.
"	29.8.16		Bn. in billets. rejoined Bn. 9th Div. Reinforcement of 51 N.C.O.s & men and 1 officer 2/Lt. T.G. Halliwell	2/3 R.W.F.
"	30.8.16		Bn. in billets. Incessant rain hindered work of training on range	2/3 R.W.F.
"	31.8.16		Bn. in billets. Training Carried out. New draft fired on Range. N.B. Working Party of 230 N.C.O.s then still with 176 Tunnelling Cy. R.E. Since 12.8.16.	R.W.F.

R.W.F. Burton Lt. R.W.F.
Lieut. Regt.

WAR DIARY
or
INTELLIGENCE SUMMARY

(Erase heading not required.)

Place	Date	Hour	Summary of Events and Information	Remarks and references to Appendices
VILLERS AU BOIS	1.9.16		Bn in billets. Training carried out. Bde Open. Order 17. Received Bn warned to move to	RMT
"	2.9.16		FRESNICOURT 2nd unit. Bn in billets. Bn moved to FRESNICOURT.	RMT
FRESNICOURT	3.9.16		Bn in billets. Bn baked. An inspection carried out.	RMT
"	4.9.16		Bn in billets. Training carried out. "A" Coy firing on range.	RMT
"	5.9.16		Bn in billets. Training carried out. "B" Coy firing on range.	RMT
"	6.9.16		Bn in billets. Training carried out. "C" Coy firing on range.	RMT
"	7.9.16		Bn in billets. Training carried out. "D" Coy firing on range.	RMT
"	8.9.16		Bn in billets. Training carried out. Divnl grenade school on range. Remainder (Coy specialists) on Route March.	RMT
"	9.9.16		Bn in billets. Training carried out in morning. Sports in afternoon. Concert in evening.	RMT
"	10.9.16		Bn in billets. Church Parade.	RMT
"	11.9.16		Bn in billets. "A" Coy on Range. "D" Bayonet fighting practice Capt B.T. Ackton. B + C. Coys Route March.	RMT
"	12.9.16		Bn in billets. "B" Coy on range. Reinforcement Capt S.A.Cameron. C + D Kit inspection.	RMT
"	13.9.16		Bn in billets. "C" Coy on Range "B" Coy " A + D Coys Route March.	RMT
"	14.9.16		Bn in billets. "D" Coy on Range. "C" Coy " A + B Coys kit inspection	RMT
"	15.9.16		Bn in billets. Worst shots of each company on Range. Remainder practice Rapid Wiring &c.	RMT
"	16.9.16		Bn moved to BOIS de la HAI.	RMT
"	17.9.16		Bn moved to SAIN and billeted there. Camerons Capt & inspection	RMT

Given a & c

WAR DIARY
INTELLIGENCE SUMMARY

Army Form C. 2118

Place	Date	Hour	Summary of Events and Information	Remarks and references to Appendices
SAIN.	18.9.16		Bn in billets. 2 Coy T.C.M. reconnoitred SOUCHEZ 2 sub section.	28 PM
"	19.9.16		Bn moved into the trenches and relieved NELSON Bn. naval Div.	PM
"	20.9.16		Bn in trenches "C" Coy Right; "B" centre "A" left. "D" in support.	PM
"	21.9.16		Bn in trenches. Capt. E.A. Cameron took over 2nd in command vice Maj. Pattinson appointed Commandant Divisional Training School	PM
"	22.9.16		" "	PM
"	23.9.16		" " Casualties 2 Lewis Gunners "D" Coy killed.	PM
"	24.9.16		Bn relieved in trenches by 10 Bn. York & Lancaster Regt.	PM
"	25.9.16		Bn in Reserve. Working parties found for work in the line 3 off. 300 O.R. 2 Platoons "D" Coy lent to 4th Middlesex Regt. and in the trenches in S.B. support & then.	PM
"	26.9.16		Bn in Billets. Capt. & adjt. P. Brown proceeded to England on leave that C.P.M. Lilly	SAC
"	27.9.16		" " Capt " " "	SAC
"	28.9.16		" " " "	SAC
"	29.9.16		" " Lt. Col. Johnston D.S.O. left for England on leave at 6 am Capt. E.A. Cameron took over Command G.O.C. (Count Gleichen) inspected the Camp.	SAC
"	30.9.16		" " "BED" A.D.C. (S.L.I.) Capt " " Bn moves into the trenches starting at 7.17 pm.	SAC

Gwun. Alameun.
Capt.
Cmdg 8: Lincolnshires

Prefix Code m.	Words	Charge	This message is on a/c of:	Recd. at m.
Office of Origin and Service Instructions	Sent At m. To By		Service. (Signature of "Franking Officer.")	Date From By

TO 37 D.W.Q

* Sender's Number. FB 120 | Day of Month First | In reply to Number | A A A

A.F.C. 2118 December 1916 please. for is this forwarded unit for Lenworth

From Lincolnshire Rgt
Place HQ
Time 2 A.M.

Lt Col.
2nd Lincolnshire Rgt

"A" Form.
MESSAGES AND SIGNALS.

Army Form C.2121
(in pads of 100).
No. of Message ....

Prefix ...... Code	Words	Charge	This message is on a/c of:	Recd. at .... m.
Office of Origin and Service Instructions	Sent		................Service.	Date ....
	At .... m.			From ....
	To			
	By		(Signature of "Franking Officer.")	By ....

TO { A Office 37 Division

Sender's Number.	Day of Month.	In reply to Number.	A A A
MB 196	31		

AFC 2118 for this unit is forwarded herewith. Please.

From Lincolnshire R
Place HQ
Time 6.30 P.M.

Lt. Col.
Comdg. Lnc R.

WAR DIARY or INTELLIGENCE SUMMARY

Army Form C. 2118

Place	Date	Hour	Summary of Events and Information	Remarks and references to Appendices
Trenches Souchez II	1/10/16		BN in trenches. Heavy hostile Minenwerfer bombarded on trenches. No casualties.	See
	2/10/16		BN in trenches. Enemy Minenwerfer very active, doing great	See
	3/10/16		BN in trenches. } damage to our trenches. No casualties	See
	4/10/16		BN in Trenches	See
	5/10/16		BN in Trenches	See
	6/10/16		BN relieved by 10th York & Lancaster Regt. 45 men supplied for working party in the trenches. Res W.D Stedman C.F. left the Bn.	See
	7/10/16		BN in billets & on working parties. Rev C.B. Throttlecke joined BN	See
	8/10/16		" " " "	See
	9/10/16		" " " " Capt J. Brown returned from leave &	See
	10/10/16		resumed duties of adjutant. BN in billets. Capt Gammon & a c/o recruited Souchez I Trench.	RM
	11/10/16		L Col J. Lanstar returned from leave & assumed command of BN	RM
	12/10/16		BN relieved 4th Bn Huddx Regt in Souchez I Sub Section Casualties: nil. BN in trenches Trenches heavily shelled with Minenwerfer. 1 Killed 4 wounded	RM
	13/10/16		" " Trenches shelled with Minenwerfer. 1 Killed 4 slightly wounded. We were unable to obtain any artillery retaliation	RM

WAR DIARY
INTELLIGENCE SUMMARY

Army Form C. 2118

Place	Date	Hour	Summary of Events and Information	Remarks and references to Appendices
Trenches Sorchez I	14/10/16		Bn in trenches. Trenches shelled with minenwerfer. 1 Severely wounded	YSL Ray
"	15/10/16		Bn in trenches. Casualties nil	YSL Ray
"	16/10/16		Bn relieved by 20th Canadian Regt. Bn marched into billets at Bruay	YSL Ray
COUPIGNY	17/10/16		Bn in billets. Men bathed & clothing be fitted. Brig Gen Hill visited Lt Col Johnston D.S.O.	YSL Ray
FREVILLIERS	18/10/16		Bn marched to billets at FREVILLIERS arriving 3 pm. Bn halted on road whilst Major Pattinson returned to Dispersal point in 19/2nd	YSL Ray
"	19/10/16		Bn in billets. Lt Col Johnston D.S.O. attended Conference at H/Q Inf Bde at CHELERS. Kit inspections etc carried out.	YSL Ray
DENIER	20/10/16		Bn marched to DENIER. L/Col Johnston DSO & the Adjutant visited the trenches	YSL Ray
AMPLIER	21/10/16		Bn marched to billets in AMPLIER.	YSL Ray
RAINCHEVAL	22/10/16		Bn marched to billets in RAINCHEVAL.	YSL Ray
"	23/10/16		Bn in billets. Kit inspections etc carried out. Lt Col Johnston DSO & Major Pattinson attended Conference at 63rd Bde HQ	YSL Ray
"	24/10/16		Bn in billets. Divisional Operation orders received from 63rd Inf Bde re attack.	YSL Ray
"	25/10/16		Bn in billets. Coy Commanders Bn bombing officer Bn Snipers officer attended conference at Bn HQ.	YSL Ray
"	26/10/16		Bn in billets. Training carried out	YSL Ray

WAR DIARY
or
INTELLIGENCE SUMMARY

(Erase heading not required.)

Army Form C. 2118

Place	Date	Hour	Summary of Events and Information	Remarks and references to Appendices
RAINCHEVAL	27/10/16		Bn in billet. Training, attack practice carried out. Lt Col Johnston D.S.O. accompanied Brig Gen E.R. Hill to MENSIL & attended a conference on 63rd Inf. Bde. HQ at 5 p.m.	
"	28/10/16		Bn in billets. Training, attack practice carried out.	
"	29/10/16		Bn in billets. Training carried out.	
"	30.10.16		Bn moved to Billets in BEAUVAL.	
BEAUVAL	31.10.16		Bn in billets. Training carried out. Incessant rain for two weeks has since stopped proper training in the open.	

R.M. Johnston
Lt Col.
Comdg 10th R.I.

WAR DIARY or INTELLIGENCE SUMMARY

Army Form C. 2118

8 Lincolns 63/31

Place	Date	Hour	Summary of Events and Information	Remarks and references to Appendices
BEAUVAL	1-11-16		in billets. Bn. Training carried out. Kit inspection.	J.B. R.M.7
"	2-11-16		Bn. in Billets. Training carried out. Route March. Staffs since 4 July 1916 trained in Anti gas appliances by Div. Gas Officer. Lecture on Gas Shells by Div. Gas Off. J.B. & men found for work under Town Major	J.B. R.M.7
"	3-11-16		Bn in Billets. Working Party of 1 OrNCO. and 80 men found for work under Town Major	J.B. R.M.7
"	3-11-16		Bn training in Attack Practice.	J.B. R.M.7
"	4-11-16		Bn in Billets. Battn. took part in Brigade Attack Practice. 8.45 a.m – 1.15 p.m.	J.B. R.M.7
"	5-11-16		Bn in Billets. Rifle inspection. Church Parades.	J.B. R.M.7
"	6-11-16		Bn in Billets. Training carried out. Route March. Refitting.	J.B. R.M.7
"	7-11-16		Bn in Billets. Incessant rain hindered training.	J.B. R.M.7
"	7-11-16		Bn moved to Billets in LUCHEUX marched 9 miles arrived LUCHEUX 4.15 P.M.	J.B. R.M.7
LUCHEUX	8-11-16		Bn in Billets. Training carried out.	J.B. R.M.7
"	9-11-16		Bn in Billets. Training carried out. Lewis Gunners firing on Range.	J.B. R.M.7
"	10-11-16		Bn in Billets. Training carried out. Bn. issued with Box Respirators	J.B. R.M.7
"	11-11-16		Bn in Billets. Fitting of Box Respirators.	J.B. R.M.7
ACHEUX	12-11-16		Bn marched to ACHEUX and were billeted in ACHEUX WOOD. in tents.	J.B. R.M.7
"	13-11-16		Bn in camp in ACHEUX WOOD. Attack by 5th Corps. on German position N. of R. ANCRE..	
"	14-11-16		Bn marched to camp near MARTINSART. arriving there at 1 p.m. left again about 7 p.m. Took over part of position captured by 63rd (Naval) Division. including part of BEAUCOURT village.	R.M.7

WAR DIARY
or
INTELLIGENCE SUMMARY

(Erase heading not required.)

Army Form C. 2118

Place	Date	Hour	Summary of Events and Information	Remarks and references to Appendices
TRENCHES	14.11.16 to 20.11.16		Bn in action commanded by Lt. Col. R.H. JOHNSTON D.S.O. Missing believed Prisoner Casualties Officers — Capt J.T. Preston & 2Lt. J.B. Higgins - wounded & 2Lt. L.R. Saunders - wounded and missing believed prisoner of war. Other Ranks. Killed 14 Wounded 115 Missing 8 Evacuated Sick - 35. 172 Total; including 34 N.C.O's	App 7 " App 7 App 7 App 7 App 7 App 7 App 7 App 7 App 7 App 7 App 7 App 7
"	21.11.16		Bn in reserve	
"	22.11.16		do	
"	23.11.16		Bn moved to trenches -	
"	24.11.16		Bn in trenches Beaumont-Hamel	
"	25.11.16		"	
"	26.11.16		Bn relieved by 21st London Regt. and marched to billets at Mailly Mailletz Bn in billets -	
MAILLY-MAILLET	27.11.16			
"	28.11.16		Bn moved to Mailly Maillet Wood encamped for night -	
"	29.11.16			
"	30.11.16		Bn moved to ACHEUX WOOD encamped for night.	

WAR DIARY
or
INTELLIGENCE SUMMARY

(Erase heading not required.)

Army Form C. 2118

8 Kinrak Rgt
Oct /5

Place	Date	Hour	Summary of Events and Information	Remarks and references to Appendices
SARTON	1.12.16		Bn moved from ACHEUX WOOD to SARTON. Billets. Refitting carried out.	
	2.12.16		Bn in Billets. Part bathed —	
	3.12.16		Church Parade. Box Respirators of 3 Corps tested in Bn in billets by Divisional gas officer. Last 3 days that actual Gas. Training carried out.	
	4.12.16		Bn in billets. Training carried out. 132 Privates without any N.C.O's drilled separately, only 5 officers & men had been out before. T All red joined Training. This large number of men arriving without any N.C.Os handicaps this Battn. after losing 34 NCOs last week; it is extremely difficult for Bn to find N.C.Os to carry on with.	
	5.12.16		Bn in billets. Training carried out.	
	6.12.16		Bn in billets. Training carried out.	
	7.12.16		Bn in billets. Training carried out. Inspection of Arms. Full Marching Order by Commanding Officer.	
	8.12.16		Bn in billets. Training carried out.	
	9.12.16		Bn in billets. Inspection of Bn. by Lt. Gen. E.A. FANSHAWE, C.B. Corps Commander. Lt. Col. R.H. Johnston D.S.O. relinquished command of Bn.	

WAR DIARY
or
INTELLIGENCE SUMMARY

(Erase heading not required.)

Army Form C. 2118

Place	Date	Hour	Summary of Events and Information	Remarks and references to Appendices
SARTON	9.2.16		MAJOR E.A. CAMERON assumed command of Bn.	2B. EAC
	10.12.16		Bn. in Billets. Church Parades.	
"	11.12.16		Bn. in Billets. Training carried out.	2.R. BM
"	12.12.16		Bn. in Billets. Training carried out. A draft of 164 joined the Battalion, including 2 Lewis Gunners & 2 Snipers.	2.R. EAC
			bombers & 2 Signallers	T.C.C
"	13.12.16		Bn in Billets. Training carried out. Battalion Parade	2.R. EAC
MEZEROLLES	14.12.16		Bn. moved to billets in MEZEROLLES. Arrived 3.20 P.M. 15 men fell out	EAC JB. SAC
CONCHY	15.12.16		Bn. moved to Billets in CONCHY. No men fell out on line of march.	J/3. ECC
HUCLIER	16.12.16		Bn. marched to HUCLIER. 4 Coys in HUCLIER and HQ Coy in BRITEL. 3 men fell out	J/3. EAC
			Bn HQ in HUCLIER	
			on line of march.	
AMETTES	17.12.16		Bn. marched to billets in AMETTES. 4 men fell out on line of march.	J/3 EAC
			No. 9/10954 Sgt. Davey C.R. and No. 58 L/Cpl. Atkinson H. candidates for commissions	
			left Bn. for England. Major Carot School.	
La PERRIERE	18.12.16		Bn. marched to billets in la PIERRIERE. No men fell out on line of march.	J/3 EAC
			Bn. HQ in PERRIERE. Bdo HQ in BUSNES. Dw. HQ. ST VENNANT.	
			No. 7370 Pte. H. STOLWORTHY a candidate for commission left Bn. for England.	COC
	19.12.16		Bn. in Billets. Refilling and cleaning of equipment carried out.	J/3. EAC
			Bn. addressed on parade by Major S.A. Cameron Officer Commanding	
	20.12.16		Bn. in billets. Refilling. Covering officer Pabol HQ. No 7 Coy Patrol.	J/3. 2.9.C

WARE DIARY or INTELLIGENCE SUMMARY

Army Form C. 2118

Place	Date	Hour	Summary of Events and Information	Remarks and references to Appendices
La PERRIERE	21.12.16		Bn. in billets. No. 1. 2. 3 Corps bathed. Commanding Officer inspected 2 Cyclo previous to their promotion. C/o attended conference at 63rd Bde. HQ. Bde O.O. 104 Received Company Commanders in conference with C/o re move on 22nd inst. Capt. Ken. 2/Lt. Buster proceeded on leave. Reinforcement of 3 officers 2/Lt. & Brown H. Tomlinson W.B. Gregory and sick other ranks.	EAC
LESTREM	22.12.16		Bn. marched to LESTREM area. Arrived 2.40 P.M. No one fell out on line of march. Billets very scattered.	EAC
"	23.12.16		Bn in billets. Training carried out. C/o attended at Div. HQ at 10 a.m. and at Bde HQ at 2.30 P.M.	JB. AM
"	24.12.16		Bn in billets. Church Parade. Organising Regt. Band.	JB. to CM
"	25.12.16		Bn in billets. Very rainy weather. Church parade not held.	
"	26.12.16		Bn in Trellis. Training carried out. 1 Off 93 unlrained men billeted in CALONNE. Sur Lys.	JB. EAC
"	27.12.16		Bn in billets. Training carried out. 2 Lt. Rushton & Lewis and 100 N.C.O.'s man billeted in HAVERSKERQUE for work on D.N. Range.	
"	28.12.16		Bn in billets. Troops reviewed by Major Gen. Simpson Colonel-in-chief of the Loyal N. Lancashire Regiment. Major T.A. Cameron appointed to the command of the Battalion with effect from 4th Gen.l hosps 16 December 1916.	EAC
"	29.12.16		Bn in billets. Box Respirator tested. Inoculation carried out.	EAC

WAR DIARY
or
INTELLIGENCE SUMMARY

(Erase heading not required.)

Army Form C. 2118

Instructions regarding War Diaries and Intelligence Summaries are contained in F.S. Regs., Part II. and the Staff Manual respectively. Title Pages will be prepared in manuscript.

Place	Date	Hour	Summary of Events and Information	Remarks and references to Appendices
LESTREM	30.12.16		Bn. in billets. Major Pattinson and Atwell adjutant and others wanted MO of Bn in support of the disposition.	
"	31.12.16		Bn in billets. Church Parade. Major Genl. H. Bruce-Williams C.B. D.S.O. Commanding 37th Division attended. Bn moved to fresh billets in VIEILLE CHAPELLE area. No men fell out on the line of march.	
VIEILLE CHAPELLE.				

V.C.6 Army Form C. 2118
8th Bn. Lincolnshire Regt

WAR DIARY
or
INTELLIGENCE SUMMARY
(Erase heading not required.)

Place	Date	Hour	Summary of Events and Information	Remarks and references to Appendices
VIEILLE CHAPELLE	1.1.17		Bn. in Billets. Other Coy rejoined Bn. from CALONNE. B Coy rejoined Bn. from HAVERSKERQUE. D.W. Rouge.	W
	2.1.17		Bn. from HAVERSKERQUE D.W. Rouge. C/O Adjutant & Coy Commanders visited H.Q. of 13 Bn. R.F. preparatory to Bn. moving into Bn in Bde. Reserve.	W
FOSSE	2.1.17		Bn in Billets. Training carried out.	W
"	3.1.17		Bn in Billets. Working Party 200 other ranks 1 Off - for work on the line. C/O and Adjutant visited No 2 Yard R.E. La GORGUE. INDENTS on C.R.E. submitted for work on the line at	W
"	4.1.17		Bn in Billets. Working Party 280 NCOs then 1 Off. for work on the line Bde. Bombing School. C/o. 2i/c Commanders and Adjutant visited 1st Army Workshop BETHUNE. Indents on C.R.E submitted Coy Commanders reconnoitred emergency routes to the line.	W
"	5.1.17		Bn. in Billets. Working Parties of 260 NCOs men. 30 Off. C.Q.M.S. & Sergt Battalion to report at Cadet School in England in Gazette. Capt. H. D. SMART R.A.M.S. Publication of New Years Honours List. Capt. B.J.L. BEARD mentioned in despatches. Awarded MILITARY CROSS G.C.M.	W
	6.1.17		Bn. in Billets. Col. E.A.CAMERON member G.C.M. Major PATTINSON 2Lt. WAUGH - Asst. ADJ. and Company Commanders visited the line and reconnoitred forenoon Making over on the 8th/Lincs.	W
	7.1.17		Bn in Billets. Working parties 30 Off. 208 men in working parties Bde Bombing School	W

WAR DIARY
or
INTELLIGENCE SUMMARY
(Erase heading not required.)

Army Form C. 2118

5th B'n Shropshire Regt

Place	Date	Hour	Summary of Events and Information	Remarks and references to Appendices
TRENCHES	8.1.17		Bn moved to the trenches in LEFT (NEUVE CHAPELLE) SECTION. A Coy. RIGHT. C Coy LEFT. B Coy left support D Coy right support. Front companies relieved by their supports after 3 days.	NR
	9-1-17		Quiet day. Good Reconnoitring by left & right Coys. 2/Lt Harrison "Tanner" Reinforcement of 3 officers 2/Lts Harrison, CM, Jenins B, Seddon C.S. arrived at NR	NR
	10.1.17		Bn in Trenches. Artillery strafe. Front-line re-instated temporarily. No casualties.	NR
	11-1-17		Bn in Trenches. Enemy T.M. active on our left. No casualties. "Gas Alert On".	NR
	12.1.17		Bn in Trenches. A very quiet day.	NR
	13.1.17		Bn in Trenches. Good Reconnoitring. C Coy. proceeded to LONDON to join CADET SCHOOL. A.C.Q.M.S. WILSON	NR
	14.1.17		Bn in Trenches. Very misty weather. Lt Col E.A. Cameron wounded. Evacuated to Base. Major D. DAVIES-EVANS assumed command of the Bn.	NR
	15.1.17		Bn moved to billets in LOCON area.	NR
LOCON area	16.1.17		Bn in Billets. Refitting of Battalion	NR

WAR DIARY
or
INTELLIGENCE SUMMARY

(Erase heading not required.)

Army Form C. 2118.

8th B⁄ⁿ Lincolnshire Regt

Place	Date	Hour	Summary of Events and Information	Remarks and references to Appendices
LOOS ON AREA	17.1.17		Bn in billets. Rations for R.E. 120 NCOs & men	AF AF
	18.1.17		Bn in billets. Training carried out.	AF AF
	19.1.17		Bn in billets. Training carried out.	AF AF
	20.1.17		Bn in billets. Training carried out.	AF AF
	21.1.17		Bn in billets. Training carried out. % inspected Coy's Marching order	AF AF
	22.1.17		Bn in billets. Training carried out.	AF AF
	23.1.17		Bn in billets. Bn inspected by Div. Commander Regt Co. H.B. Walker	AF AF
			C.B. D.T.O.	
	24.1.17		Bn in billets. Training carried out	AF
	25.1.17		Capt. Aquith visited line preparatory to taking over	AF AF
	26.1.17		Capt. R.S.M. visited H.Q. of different Bns. Preparatory to taking over	AF AF
	27.1.17		Bn took part in Bde Exercise - Infantry & Aeroplane Co-opration	AF AF
	28.1.17		Bn moved into nuthen area under staff with tea. Bn in tents	AF AF

SDE

Army Form C. 2118

WAR DIARY
or
INTELLIGENCE SUMMARY

(Erase heading not required.)

5th Bn. Lincolnshire Regt.

Place	Date	Hour	Summary of Events and Information	Remarks and references to Appendices
TRENCHES	29.6.17		Bn in Trenches no casualties	HP MR
"	30.6.17		Bn in Trenches "	HP MR
"	31.6.17		Bn in Trenches "	HP MR

Selwin Dane Secund
Lt Col
5th Lincolnshire Regt.

To 37 Dn- D.

Herewith AF. 2118 for the month of February 1917. for the 8th Bn. The Lincolnshire Regt.

28/2/17.

H Stacey Clifford Lt. Col.
Lincolnshire Regt.

WAR DIARY or INTELLIGENCE SUMMARY

Army Form C. 2118

8 Lincolns pg 27
62

VII/17

Place	Date	Hour	Summary of Events and Information	Remarks and references to Appendices
TRENCHES	1/2/17		B^n relieved by 1st Bn NORFOLK REGT. & went into Billets in BETHUNE	YMW
BETHUNE	2/2/17		B^n in billets. Training carried out	YMW
	3/2/17		B^n in billets. French lesson of 25 picking platoon commenced	YMW
	4/2/17		2/Lt TOLHURST.B & 2/Lt SMITH F.W. joined B^n - Church Parade	YMW
	5/2/17		B^n in billet. Training carried out	JB
	6/2/17		B^n in billets. Training carried out	JB
	7/2/17		B^n in billets. Training carried out	JB
	8/2/17		B^n in billets. Training carried out	JB
	9/2/17		B^n in billets. Training carried out	JB
	10/2/17		Lt. Col. T Astley Cubitt C.M.G. D.S.O. reported and took command of the Bn. v^ce B^n Major D Davies. Some to 8th Bn Somerset L. Infantry. Capt & Asst D. Barron rejoined B^n from leave and assumed duties of adjutant.	JB
	11.2.17		2/c Adjutant attended Church Parade	
MAZINGARBE	12.2.17		B^n moved to billets in MAZINGARBE	
	13.2.17		B^n moved into Fm in support relieved 4th Bn Middlesex Regt	JB

WAR DIARY
or
INTELLIGENCE SUMMARY
(Erase heading not required.)

Army Form C. 2118

Instructions regarding War Diaries and Intelligence Summaries are contained in F.S. Regs., Part II. and the Staff Manual respectively. Title Pages will be prepared in manuscript.

Place	Date	Hour	Summary of Events and Information	Remarks and references to Appendices
TRENCHES.	14/2/17		Bn in Trenches. Trenches reconnoitred. Party of 10ff + 50 other ranks attached to 152 Coy. R.E.	JB
"	15/2/17		Bn in Trenches. Transport dismounted H.Q. fire in L00s 2 L.D. lines wounded.	JB
"	16/2/17		Bn in Trenches. All available men utilised in cleaning trenches and burying loose kits etc.	JB
"	17/2/17		Bn in trenches. Commanding Offr. 2/c Company commanders reconnoitred front line trenches. Brigadier visited C/O. Div. Commander visited C/O.	JB
"	18/2/17		Bn in Trenches. one man wounded.	JB
"	19/2/17		Bn in trenches. Capt. H. HUSSEY SOMERSET LIGHT INFANTRY joined Bn as acting 2/c. Major H. PATTINSON assumed command of No 4 Coy.	JB
"	20.2.17		Bn in Trenches. No 3 Coy. Right front with No 1 Coy in support. No 2 Coy Left front with No 4 Coy in support.	JB
"	21.2.17		Bn in Trenches. Good patrol work done by Capt Cordner M.C. 7 Tpl Platt.	JB
"	22.2.17		Bn in Trenches	JB
"	23.2.17		Bn in Trenches No 3 Coy (Capt. Harrison) moved into MAZINGARBE. No 4 Coy Yorks (Lancaster became Coy. in R. support.	JB
"	24.2.17		Bn in Trenches.	JB

WAR DIARY
or
INTELLIGENCE SUMMARY

Army Form C. 2118

Place	Date	Hour	Summary of Events and Information	Remarks and references to Appendices
MAZINGARBE	25-2-17		Bn. relieved by 10 Bn. YORK & LANCASTER REGT. and moved into billets in MAZINGARBE. Worken defences. (1 Coy. No 3 Coy)	JB.
"	26.2.17		Bn in Billets. Work on defences (2 Coy No 2 & 3 Coy)	JB.
"	27-2-17		Bn in Billets. Work on defences (3 Coy No 1, 2, & 4 Coy) Bn	JB.
"	28.2.17		Bn in Billets. Work on defences.	JB.

WAR DIARY
or
INTELLIGENCE SUMMARY

(Erase heading not required.)

Army Form C. 2118

8 Lincoln Regt. Vol 1/8

Place	Date	Hour	Summary of Events and Information	Remarks and references to Appendices
MAZINGARBE	1/3/16		Bn in Billets. Officers attended demonstration of new attack by Bn of 111th Bde. O.O. 107 published regarding move on the 2nd inst.	J.B.
BETHUNE	2-3-16		Bn marched to Billets in BETHUNE.	J.B.
ROBECQ	3-3-16		Bn marched to Billets in ROBECQ.	J.B.
BOERECQ	4-3-16		Bn marched to BOERECQ and billeted itself. Billets in ST HILAIRE taken by 112th Bde.	J.B.
"	5-3-17		Bn in Billets: New organisation effected: Coys. practised in new organisation parades.	J.B.
"	6-3-17		Bn in Billets. Training carried out. Inspection by Commanding Officer.	J.B.
"	7-3-17		Bn in Billets. Training carried out. New organisation	J.B.
"	8-3-17		Bn in Billets. Training carried out.	J.B.
TANGRY	9-3-17		Bn moved to Billets in TANGRY.	
NEUVILLE AU CORNET	10-3-17		Bn moved to Billets in NEUVILLE-au-CORNET. 3 Coys & HQrs. NEUVILLE 1 Coy in TACHINCOURT.	J.B.
"	11-3-17		Bn rested.	J.B.
"	12-3-17		Bn in Billets. Training carried out. Major J.W. Seabrook assumed duties of 2nd in Command. Major W. Lucecarolyse Regt. on route March.	J.B.
"	13-3-17		Bn in Billets. Training on Coys training grounds.	J.B.
"	14-3-17		Bn in Billets	J.B.

Army Form C. 2118

WAR DIARY
or
INTELLIGENCE SUMMARY
(Erase heading not required.)

Instructions regarding War Diaries and Intelligence Summaries are contained in F. S. Regs., Part II. and the Staff Manual respectively. Title Pages will be prepared in manuscript.

Place	Date	Hour	Summary of Events and Information	Remarks and references to Appendices
NEUVILLE au CORNET.	15/3/17		Bn in billets. Training carried out. — Letting and preparing Bombing Ground	J.B.
"	16-3-17		Bn in Billets. "B" Coy firing on Range.	J.B.
"	17-3-17		Bn in Billets. Training carried out; Recreational training in afternoon.	J.B.
"	18.3.17		Bn. Batted except Hq. Coy. Voluntary Church Parades.	J.B.
"	19-3-17		Bn. Route march. — MAISNIL., OCOCHE., HERLIN., FRAMECOURT., FT. HOUVIN., MONCHEAUX; MONT-EN-TERROIS.	J.B.
"	20.3.17		Commanding Officer visited ARRAS. — reconnoitred. Orders to commence training very difficult. Received notice to be ready to move with 6 hrs notice.	J.B.
"	21.3.17		Bn in Billets. Training carried out.	J.B.
"	22.3.17		" " " Sgt. GODDARD J proceeded to England to join Cadet School.	J.B.
"	23.3.17		Bn. marched to "I" Corps Training Ground and carried out attack practise. Dinners taken on the Ground.	J.B.
"	24.3.17		Bn in Billets. Training carried out under Company arrangements. Recreational Training in the afternoon.	J.B.

WAR DIARY
or
INTELLIGENCE SUMMARY

(Erase heading not required.)

Army Form C. 2118

Place	Date	Hour	Summary of Events and Information	Remarks and references to Appendices
NEUVILLE AU CORNET	25-3-17		Church Parade by Coys. Final of Bn. Football Tournament. H.Q.Coy v. D Coy.	JB
"	26-3-17		Bn Route March. Very wet day. Commanding Off. attended conference at Corps H.Q.	JB
"	27-3-17		Bn in Billets. Training carried out.	JB
"	28-3-17		Bn in Billets. Two Coy. firing on range. Major H. Pattinson	JB
"	29-3-17		Bn on Route March (Hdrs & Coy. 'C' Coy on Range.) DUNEVILLE; MONCHEAUX; SIBIVILLE, outskirts FREVENT; HOUVIN HOUVIGNEUL; Bombing R. Grenade etc.	JB
"	30-3-17		Bn in Billets. Training carried out. Joining on Range. Commanding Off. attended conference at Bde. H.Q.	JB
"	31-3-17		Bn in Billets. Training carried out.	JB

T. Ashley Cubitt
Lt Colonel
O.C. 8th Lincoln Regt

31/3/17

Quiechshire Regt.

205. To 137 Div Q

Herewith A.F.C 2118 for
month of April 1917 please

[stamp: 27A 1 MAY 1917 HEADQUARTERS]

Scrowley Adjt
Quiechshire Regt

Army Form C. 2118

WAR DIARY
or
INTELLIGENCE SUMMARY
(Erase heading not required.)

8th Bn. (Lancashire) Regt.   Vol 19   37/63

Place	Date	Hour	Summary of Events and Information	Remarks and references to Appendices
NEUVILLE AU CORNET	1/4/17		Bn. in billets. Voluntary Church Parade	B.
"	2/4/17		Bn. Route March to DENIER. Attack on trench system.	C.
"	3/4/17		Bn. bathed at AVESNES LE COMTE.	H.
GIVENCHY	5/4/17		Bn. moved to GIVENCHY LE NOBLE. CHM T.A Clatterburg Q.O. 4th Bn. & Seaforth assumed Coy 5 of Bn. Bn. Greatwood Lancashire Regt. Bn. commanded by Major J.M Greatwood Lancashire Regt.	
LATTRE ST QUENTIN	7/4/17		Bn. moved to LATTRE ST QUENTIN and billeted there	
DUISANS	8/4/17		Bn. moved to DUISANS and was billeted for night. for crew	
			Bn. moved. Showers etc from Bde. Dump. Comb. Offr attended Conference at Bde. HQ. Bn. moved into ARRAS assembly area 12 noon - thence to Battery Valley. See appendices marked 1.	
ARRAS	9/4/17		Bn. attached Canadians. Advance commenced by Infantry J.M. Greatwood Canadian Offering Monad 9, Mar Parche. 1/8 Sworth 187 Trench & Bn. withdrawn from Line and moved into ARRAS.	Attache...
DUISANS	13/4/17		Bn. DUISANS and billets here. no night.	

WAR DIARY or INTELLIGENCE SUMMARY

Army Form C. 2118

Place	Date	Hour	Summary of Events and Information	Remarks and references to Appendices
BEAUFORT.	14.4.17.		Bn. moved ₼killed in BEAUFORT	
"	16.4.17		Bn. in billets. Major P. Davies-Evans appointed Cmdg. Officer. Major H. Tracey 2 i/c.	
"	17.4.17		Bn. in billets. Training Carried out.	JB
"	18.4.17		" " " "	JB
"	19.4.17		Bn. moved to killed in MONTENESCOURT.	JB
"	20.4.17		Bn. moves by buses to ARRAS. — Bn. in Support.	
ARRAS.	28.4.17.		Bn. in attack. Middlesex left front Bn. York & Lancaster Regt left front Bn. Somerset L.I. Bn. right support Bn. Warwickshire Regt. left support Bn. Casualties 2 Officers killed 2/Lt W. Dickinson 2/Lt J.R. Buxton. O.R. 20 killed. 20 Officers wounded. Lt W.B. Gregory. Wounded. Moved at 10.2. Present 162. Missing Bn. no roster.	JB
"	29.4.17.		Bn. in attack. Left of late front. Casualties. Officers Missing. 2/Lt H. Bridges. Present 22. Other Ranks Killed 22. Wounded 164. Present 105.	
ARRAS.	29.4.17.		2/Lt. H. Bridges. Bn. withdrawn from line and rested in ARRAS. Hence conveyed by Motor bus to BEAUFORT.	
BEAUFORT.	30.4.17.		Bn. in billets. Commanding Officers inspection Brig. Gen. Challoner D.S.O. Cmdg. 63rd Inf. Bde. also addressed Bn. on recent action engagement.	

Appendix 1.

8TH BATTALION, THE LINCOLNSHIRE REGIMENT.

THE BATTLE OF ARRAS.

April 9th to 12th inclusive.

1. At 5.45 pm. April 9th The Battalion left DUISANS.
    A Coy 120 O. R.
    B Coy 130 O. R.
    C Coy 156 O. R. and 3 L. G. teams who were attached to Hd.Qrs.
    D Coy of 100 O. R. was detailed as a carrying party.
    Batch. H. Q. 72.   Total Officers 17.   Other Ranks 499.

2. The Battalion marching along the ST. POL – ARRAS Road, picked up entrenching tools, passed through PORTE BAUDIMONT – ARRAS over the Railway BRIDGE across the CEMETERY to the ASSEMBLY TRENCHES at G.30.a.
   This was about 12 noon Ap. 9th.

3. About 4 pm. we moved in Art. formation to BATTERY VALLEY H.26.b. where we halted until 8 pm. and dug in.

4. From here we advanced EAST

    B. Coy.   A. Coy.   8th Som. L. I.

    C. Coy.

5. About 12 midnight Ap. 9 – 10 we halted about H.29.c.

6. Ap. 10th about 1 am. owing to the SOM. L. I. extending their front northwards B. Coy, 8th LINCOLNSHIRE REGT. moved to C. Coy's left, A Coy moved to B. Coy's left.
   A. Coy's position was then about H.29.b.

7. The previous formation had been.

    C. COY.
    B. COY.
    A. COY.
    SOM. L. I.

8. At daybreak from N.35.a. considerable enemy activity was observed round MONCHY-LE-PREUX, also enemy troops and transport moving N. E. from ROEUX.
   Artillery was asked for in each case but there was no response.

9. At 9 am. the Battalion prepared to advance to its original objective I.25.d. as soon as the 111th Bde advanced on MONCHY.

10. At 10.30 am. Major Greatwood was informed that the 8th Som. L. I. were in MONCHY and that he must support them.

11. We advanced A. Coy on right, B. Coy on left, B. Coy in support to the valley H.36.a. In this advance we suffered heavy

(1).

casualties, as we had no artillery support.

12. At 4 pm. Major Brentwood issued orders to attack MONCHY. 8 SOM. L.I. were on the right 6 LINCOLNS on the left. Again we had no artillery support and had to dig in on the high ground H.36.d.-b.

13. We here received orders to attack MONCHY at dusk.

14. Formation. Middlesex.   B. Coy.   A. Coy.   Som. L.I.
                                    C. Coy.
                                    Lincolns.

15. When already opened out for the attack, orders arrived from Bde cancelling it and giving instructions to consolidate H.36.a. Patrols were posted in front meantime.

April 11th.

16. The 15th Div. passed through us and took MONCHY shortly after the Cavalry came over ORANGE HILL and passed to our right.

17. At 12 noon, I arrived and took command. At 2 pm. I received Orders to attack and consolidate the line KEELING-COPSE - BOIS de AUBEPINES.

18. My left Coy supported the Y. & Lancs and my right Coy supported the MIDDLESEX.

19. I found before I had got far that I was E. of the YORK & Lancs and so as I was supporting I dug, and waited to see if they could get on any further.

20. They were unable to further their advance and so I dug in at H.36.b. being in touch with the Y. & L. on my left and holding a line about 400 yds to the S where I was in touch with the MIDDLESEX on my right.

Ap. 12th.

21. I continued to hold this line being subject all the time to very heavy shell and M.G. fire. This latter came from the direction of the R. SCARPE and in rear of the line PELVES - KEELING-COPSE, but although I had observers out they were unable to locate it.

22. About 5.30pm. a Battn of the W. Yorks went through to try and make good our original objective.

23. At 8 pm. I brought the Battn out without further casualties. My total casualties as far as at present ascertained are Officers 9. O.R. 240.

24. I beg to state that paras 1 - 16 inclusive were reported to me by summaries taken from O.C. Coys.

                                        Major.
                                        8th Bn. Lincolnshire Regt.

16. 4. 17.

War Diary
8th Lincolnshire Regt
May 1917

WAR DIARY or INTELLIGENCE SUMMARY

Army Form C. 2118

Place	Date	Hour	Summary of Events and Information	Remarks and references to Appendices
BEAUFORT	1/5/17		Bn. in billets. Reorganisation carried out.	JB
"	2/5/17		Bn. in billets. Evans inspected draft of 2/8 Others ranks which joined the Bn. JB. Commanding Officer Lt. Col. D. Davies and were hotel to Corps. 2/Lt J.J. HANSELL rejoined Bn. after being evacuated wounded during recent fighting.	JB
"	3/5/17		C.O. attended conference at Bde. HQ. Bn. organised re-equipped. Much artillery required in new draft.	JB
"	4/5/17		Bn. in billets. Training carried out under company arrangements.	JB
"	5/5/17		Bn. in billets. Visit of Army Commander Genl. Sir Edmund Allenby K.C.B. and Div. Commander. Major Genl. Bruce Williams C.B. D.S.O.	JB
"	6/5/17		Bde Church Parade. Brig. Genl. Challoner D.S.O. present. Commanding Officer (Lt. Col. D. Davies-Evans) attended conference at Bde HQ. 10. Reinforcement 1 Off. 2/Lt Cain and 2 O.R.	JB
"	7/5/17		Bn. in billets. "D" Coy firing on Range. Training carried out. "specials". Instructed in Lewis Gun bombing.	JB

Selwn Davies Lt Col
O.C. 8th Line

WAR DIARY or INTELLIGENCE SUMMARY

Army Form C. 2118

Place	Date	Hour	Summary of Events and Information	Remarks and references to Appendices
BEAUFORT	8/5/17		Bn. in billets. Training carried out.	JB.
"	9.5.17.		Divisional Transport Competition. 'A' Coy found in Range. 'C' Coy throwing live bombs.	JB.
"	10.5.17		Inspection of Regimental Transport by Col. Humphreys 1/c. 39th Bn. Train. Bde. Reconnoitring Exercise. Commanding Officer 2/c. 1st Coy and JB. 1 Offr. per Coy attended.	JB.
"	11.5.17		Bn. in billets. Training carried out.	JB.
"	12.5.17.		Attack Practice by 3 Coys. One Coy. on range. Lecture to all NCOs by Commanding Officer (Lt. Col. D. Dewar-Durie)	JB.
"	13.5.17.		Church Parade with 8th Bn. Somerset L.I.	JB.
"	14.5.17.		Bn. for rest in Bde. Tactical scheme.	JB.
"	15.5.17	10.0	Reinforcement. Lt. M.G. Rowcroft and 2.O.R. Bde Tactical Scheme. Lieut H.P. Smith, Acting Adjt. 6 Musders Conference at Bde HQ.	MR Selius Dawe war JC & L&&P

WAR DIARY
or
INTELLIGENCE SUMMARY
(Erase heading not required.)

Army Form C. 2118

Place	Date	Hour	Summary of Events and Information	Remarks and references to Appendices
BEAUPORT	16.5.17		Bde Tactical Scheme. (Stopped by rain). GOC 63rd Bde. (Brig Gen. E.L. Challoner D.S.O.) inspects Bn. Reinforcement. 3.O.R.	M.R.
	17.5.17		Bde Tactical Scheme (stopped by rain). Lieut Gen. Sir Ivor MAXSE visits area, & inspects battalion on parade.	M.R. M.R.
	18.5.17		Bn moved to SIMENCOURT.	M.R.
	19.5.17		Bn moved to DAINVILLE	M.R.
	20.5.17		Church Parade in morning. Company training in afternoon.	M.R.
	21.5.17		Bn moved to ARRAS.	M.R.
ARRAS	22.5.17		Bn parades by Companies. Bathe in afternoon. Evening training.	M.R.
	23.5.17		Parades, morning specialist training, Lewis gunners on range. Afternoon inter Coy company arrangements. Reinforcements 2.O.R.	M.R.
	24.5.17		Parades. Attack by Platoons on Strong points (9, 2b, c + d) Lewis gunners on range. Reinforcements: 2/Lieutenant D. Whitham 2/Lt P.J.A. Brown, 4/Lt H.N.E. W.A. WELLS-COLE expected to join Bn A/Maj Batalis Whitham assumed command & part of B Coy vice 2/Lt W. Hunter.	M.R.
	25.5.17		Parades. Training line of Outposts (9.24 + 25) Afternoon Company parades. A Company provided working party 100 men at 2 pm. Returned 7 pm. B Coy field	M.R.
	26.5.17		Transport. Attack by Companies on strong point. C. Coy on range. Reinforcements 1 NCO + O.R.	M.R.

1875. Wt. W593/826 1,000,000 4/15 J.B.C. & A. A.D.S.S./Forms/C. 2118.

Army Form C. 2118.

WAR DIARY
or
INTELLIGENCE SUMMARY.
(Erase heading not required.)

Instructions regarding War Diaries and Intelligence Summaries are contained in F. S. Regs. Part II. and the Staff Manual respectively. Title pages will be prepared in manuscript.

Place	Date	Hour	Summary of Events and Information	Remarks and references to Appendices
ARRAS	27.5.17		Church Parade. Quartermasters Stores moved to AEHICOURT	WR
	28.5.17		Morning Kit Inspection. Working party 50 men 8 a.m. Returned 1 p.m. Carpenter parades in afternoon	WR
	29.5.17		Working party 200 men. "D" Company on range. Remainder on Training ground.	WR
	30.5.17		Parades under Companies "B" & "C" Companies on range	WR
	31.5.17		Battalion on Training ground. "A" & "D" Companies on range.	WR

War diary

8th Lincolns

June 1917

MESSAGES AND SIGNALS.

Army Form C.2121
(in pads of 100).

TO 37th Division

Sender's Number: R549
Day of Month: 3
AAA

Attached is War Diary 8th Lincolns sent to this office in error

From: 63 Inf Bde

H.C. Brown Capt

WAR DIARY or INTELLIGENCE SUMMARY

Army Form C. 2118.

Place	Date	Hour	Summary of Events and Information	Remarks and references to Appendices
BEAUFORT	1.6.17		Battalion moved to BEAUFORT by bus transport (from ARRAS) at 5 p.m. Transport moved off at 8 a.m. Lt H.F. Smith & wiring party (9 men) returned to Battalion.	MR
	2.6.17		Parades in Battalion Training ground. No parade in afternoon. Reinforcements 3 officers (2nd Lt M. STUART MENTEITH, 2nd Lt J.G. SUTCLIFFE, 2nd Lt R.H. WESTOBY) & 3 O.R. 6 men returned to duty.	MR
	3.6.17		A, B, C Companies fired on Bde range at 500 yards, commencing 7 a.m. New draft inspected by C.O. at 2.30 p.m.	MR
	4.6.17		D Company on Batt'n range, remainder Company Training and Rapid Wiring Course. Kit inspection in afternoon.	MR
CROISETTE	6.6.17		Batt'n moved by bus transport to CROISETTE, starting at 9 a.m.	MR
HEUCHIN	6.6.17		Batt'n marched to HEUCHIN starting at 8 a.m.	MR
FRUGES	7.6.17		Batt'n marched to FRUGES starting at 11.30 a.m.	MR
	8.6.17		Company Commanders had Companies for training etc. Company of Commanding Officers at Bde HQ at 5 p.m. Capt. F.A. WAUGH, M.C. returned from leave.	MR
RADINGHEM	9.6.17		Battalion moved at 2 p.m. to RADINGHEM. Reinforcements (including details) 75 joined battalion. 2nd Lt HUNTER rejoined from Bde School at ACHIECOURT. Officers	MR

Helme Davis Evans Lt Col
O.C. 5th Lincolns

WAR DIARY
or
INTELLIGENCE SUMMARY.

Army Form C. 2118.

Place	Date	Hour	Summary of Events and Information	Remarks and references to Appendices
RADINGHEM	9.6.17		Officer reinforcements - 6, 2nd Lt A. LINTON (South Staff.) TIMPSON.N., BEALES.P.C., COPEMAN.W.H., ASKEY.C.H.L., MAJOR W.H.; Battalion bivouacked.	M.R.
	10.6.17		CHURCH Parade at 9.30 a.m.	M.R.
	11.6.17		Battalion moved into billets in village. Construction of Training grounds, range, bombing etc. Reinforcement 1 officer 2nd Lt H LEE and 31 O.R.	M.R.
	12.6.17		Battalion paraded under Company arrangements. Lecture by Brigadier Gen. P. & B. Radcliffe B.S.O. B.G. G.S. at Bde H.Q. BOMY. Reinforcements 1 officer 2nd Lt H. STONE and 120 O.R.	M.R.
	13.6.17		Battalion fired on Bde Range at HEZECAVES. Lecture at Bde Hq by Lt C.E. WEBBER. BSOM. in morning. Bn. trained on Bn Parade Ground. 'A' Company fired on Bn Range.	M.R.
	14.6.17		Batt. practised attack by 3 Companies on wood S. of RADINGHEM, 1 Company defending.	M.R.
	15.6.17		Afternoon Specialist etc. Training. Reinforcements 1 officer 2nd Lt WILLIAMS J.R.	M.R.
	16.6.17		Specialist & Company Training in morning. B Coy on range. Reinforcements 1 officer 2nd Lieut. J. R. McDONNELL. (No parade in afternoon)	M.R.
	17.6.17		Church Parade 9.30 a.m. Voluntary Bathing party, A & B Coys at 2 p.m., C & D Coys at 5 p.m. M.R.	
	18.6.17		Battalion trained in morning on Training grounds. B Company on Bn Range. 10 p.m. an Lewis Gun Coy Lt. St. Aubin	

O C El Aubin

WAR DIARY
or
INTELLIGENCE SUMMARY.

Army Form C. 2118.

Place	Date	Hour	Summary of Events and Information	Remarks and references to Appendices
RADINGHEM	19.6.17		Battalion fired on Bde Range at HEZECQUES. Bde Armourer commenced inspecting rifles, Lewis guns & Triangles.	
	20.6.17		Weather uncertain. Batt: trained in morning on Bn Parade Ground.	M.R
	21.6.17		Holiday. Bde Sports at FRUGES.	M.R
RELY	22.6.17		Battalion marched to RELY starting 9 a.m. 1 man fell out.	M.R
STEENBECQUE	23.6.17		Battalion marched to STEENBECQUE, starting 5.45 a.m. No men fell out	M.R
CAESTRE	24.6.17		Battalion marched to CAESTRE. Starting 4.30 a.m. No men fell out	M.R
BRULOOZE	25.6.17		Battalion marched to M'Camp near BRULOOZE, starting 6.15 a.m. 1 man fell out	M.R
"	26.6.17		Battalion rested. Lecture to officers by C.O. Conference of Comndg. Officers at Bde HQ.	M.R
"	27.6.17		Company parades. C.O. & C/Leaders reconnoitre trenches.	M.R
"	28.6.17		Company Parades.	M.R
TRENCHES	29.6.17		Batt. moved into trenches at O.8 + O.14 (Map WYTSCHAETE 28.S.W 2.1/10,000), B + C Coys in advance. A + D in rear. Batt: took over from the Middlesex Regt. who moved into front line (left sub section) Bn HQ at ZERO WOOD) 2 Offrs Reinforcement 3 Officers (Capt A.B. WIGGINS, 2Lt J. MULLOCK, 2Lt J. TUNNEY + 6 other ranks jd. Salvage parties. Working party of 20 men sent to Mx Regt. No casualties.	M.R
"	B.6.17			

John David Lyon Lt. Col.
O.C. 8th Division

War Diary
1st Lincolns
July 1917

"A" Form.
MESSAGES AND SIGNALS.

Army Form C.2121
(in pads of 100.)
No. of Message _____

Prefix _____ ode _____ m.	Words	Charge	This message is on a/c of:	Recd. at _____ m.
Office of Origin and Service Instructions.	Sent		_____ Service.	Date _____
	At _____ m.			From _____
	To			
	By		(Signature of "Franking Officer.")	By _____

TO | 63rd Infy Bde

Sender's Number	Day of Month.	In reply to Number.	A A A
*R 16	3		

Herewith War Diary for July. aaa
Delay in delivery is regretted.

From | 8th Lincoln Regt.
Place
Time

The above may be forwarded as now corrected. (Z) _____
Censor.   Signature of Addresser or person authorised to telegraph in his name.

* This line should be erased if not required.
(7107) Wt. W12093/M1217 50,000 pads. 1/17. D.D.&L. (E764.) Forms C/2121/11.

WAR DIARY
or
INTELLIGENCE SUMMARY.
(Erase heading not required.)

Army Form C. 2118.

Place	Date	Hour	Summary of Events and Information	Remarks and references to Appendices
TRENCHES	1.7.17		Situation quiet. Working party 200 men with 4th Mx Regt. Wiring party 20 men. Salvage party 20 men. No casualties. Major Qu. C.B. Williams visited trenches.	MR
Mt KEMMEL	2.7.17		Relieved by 8th N. Staffs at 4 pm. Batt marched to (about) N.35.6.8.9 where batt went into camp.	MR
"	3.7.17		Battalion rested. 10 pm working party 300 men to work in line. Bathe	MR
"	4.7.17		Working party 200 men at 10 pm. 2 Casualties (1 at 4 am) A, B + half	MR
"	5.7.17		C Coy had baths at DRANOUTRE. Lt EYDEN, Belgian Interpreter joins Batt.	MR
"	6.7.17		Working party 200 men at 6 am. D Coy at baths. Working party 10 pm 50 men. Paulhumus for 8 O R	MR
"	6.7.17		Working party. Salvage 50 men, + 25 men by day, 200 by night. Conference of Company	MR
"			Officers at Bde H.Q. at 9.30 am.	MR
"	7.7.17		Working parties 175 by day 100 men at night. 1 Casualty.	MR
"	8.7.17		Working parties 275 by day	MR
"	9.7.17		Working party 260 by day. Capture of County Munro at Bde Hd.	MR
TRENCHES	10.7.17		Bn relieved 13th KRRC in Left Support Trenches. Bn HQ. TORREKEN FARM. Conference	MR
			6.10 am at Bd Htr. Casualties Nil. Sunny Slight shelling 10 pm 1.52 am	MR
"	11.7.17		Bn relieved by 4th Middlesex. Bn relieved 13th R.B. in Left Front sector. Dry	ASE

WAR DIARY
or
INTELLIGENCE SUMMARY.

Army Form C. 2118.

Place	Date	Hour	Summary of Events and Information	Remarks and references to Appendices
TRENCHES	11.7.17		Left front B Coy left support, A Coy right front, C Coy right support. Bn HQ at DERRY HOUSE. A & C By HQ at LINCOLN LODGE B & D HQ at MAHIEU FARM	
"	12.7.17		Reinforcements 1 Officer Capt R.G. CORDINER, M.C. + 5 O.R. Casualties 2 wounded. M.R. Conference of C.O.'s in Bn HQ. Visit by Brig. Gen. @ Challener. Visits Bn. Working party 100 men from support coy joined up shell holes + improving front line. No casualties. M.R.	
"	13.7.17		2nd Lt F.W.A. BROWN + 3 men patrolled towards O 23.d 02.5.3. Large working party overheard German patrol offenced moving towards RIFLE FARM. 11pm heavy enemy barrage on WAMBEKE Valley and along OOSTAVERNE road; during relief of left half batt. by 4th Middlesex. Party of enemy attacked our two posts S of Railway at O 25.c.1.2 at daybreak were repulsed. B Coy relieved A Coy when went into Rear Support line. Casualties to whom 2 Officers Capt SHART M.C. RAMC, and 2nd Lt F.W.A.BROWN (slight) 12 O.R. and 2 O.R. missing. M.R.	
"	14.7.17		Spasmodic shelling at mid-day and 2.30 pm. Barrage on WAMBEKE VALLEY at 8.50 – 9.20 p and again 11.30 pm. Working party 60 men on front sheltote line 3 Casualties (wounded) M.R.	
"	15.7.17		Visit by Brig. Gen. Challener at 6 pm. Trinity Quiet day + night. 80 men works on shell hole line N of railway and new RE trench sort of railway. 4th Mx Regt took over on left outpost. B Company moved up and took over half front line	

208

Army Form C. 2118.

WAR DIARY
or
INTELLIGENCE SUMMARY.

(Erase heading not required.)

Instructions regarding War Diaries and Intelligence Summaries are contained in F. S. Regs. Part II. and the Staff Manual respectively. Title pages will be prepared in manuscript.

Place	Date	Hour	Summary of Events and Information	Remarks and references to Appendices
TRENCHES.	15/7/17		from D. Coy. (on right) (D Coy) C Coy took over from "B" Coy, but did not move from present position. Casualties nil.	M.R.
"	14/7/17		Working parties 170 men. Patrol night 15/16th 2/Lt DOWES + S.O.R. Casualties nil.	M.R.
"	17/7/17		Working party 80 men. Enemy artillery active 9.30pm. Our artillery fired 9.50pm-12m/n to officers 24 OR 11.15 Warywide spent night in while Casualties nil.	S.O.R M.R.
"	18/7/17	2.30am	Quiet day & night. (30 men on working party. Casualties 1 missing (R.Ly) to Casualty	M.R
"	19/7/17		Bn relieved by 11th R Warwicks. and marched back to old line on KEMMEL HILL	M.R
KEMMEL HILL	20.7.17		Batt's rested. Conference of Commdg Officers at Bde H.Q.	M.R
"	21.7.17		Batt: had baths. Inspection by C.O. C.O held conference of Officers	Inf
"	22.7.17		Church parade. Batt's practised attack near camp in afternoon.	M.R
"	23.7.17		Brigade practised attack east of LINDENHOEK. Div¹ & Bde Commander present.	M.R
"	24.7.17		Batt practised attack EAST of LINDENHOEK	M.R
TRENCHES	25.7.17		Batt. relieved 11ᶠ R Warwick R. in front line trenches (inside left battalion)	M.R
"	26.7.17		Batt. relieved by 13th KRRC. GOC 63rd Bde visits line. Casualties 3.	M.R
KEMMEL HILL	27.7.17		Batt's rested.	M.R
"	28.7.17		Batt. practised attack near camp. Conference of Commanding Officers at Bde H.Q.	M.R

Place	Date	Hour	Summary of Events and Information	Remarks and references to Appendices
TRENCHES KEMMEL	29.7.17		Batt. relieved 13th KRRC in front line. Casualties 3 (2 wounded 1 killed.)	MR
"	30.7.17		Batt. HQ moved to Lincoln Lodge. B.D. assembled in front line. Shells H.Q. line. A+C in front line. Casualties 3.	WR
"	31.7.17		British attack commenced. Middlesex attacked in direction of Rifle Farm. D Coy 85 rushes forming defensive flank in rear. At 7.50 a.m. an attack began on our front. B Company attacks supported by C. Objective (this July FARM through WAR FARM to WAMBEKE RIVER) was reached, and connection established with bound on right. No pace was found by Middlesex. D Coy. MAY FARM offers resistance and left defensive flank was found by C Company, who also reinforced front line. A Company advanced to SHELTER line. 1 Coy of Middlesex, with 1 platoon A Company attacks MAY FARM unsuccessfully. 2 Lieut S HUNTER killed in this attack. Situation remained unchanged till 5 p.m., when 119th Brit Lives attacked on M.G. line. After some fighting this Battalion maintains connection on their right to SAFE flank. C Company still held on to advance to their own left. of MAY FARM with C Company left, but fails to advance during the Afternoon, remaining in SHELL hole line. Situation remains unchanged at BAS FARM and in BEEK WOOD. Another enemy attempts to counter attack	W.R.

WAR DIARY
or
INTELLIGENCE SUMMARY.

Army Form C. 2118.

Place	Date	Hour	Summary of Events and Information	Remarks and references to Appendices
TRENCHES	14.7.17		during morning officers were disposed by an artillery fire. Excellent visibility signally maintained between Battalion headquarters and forward lines was maintained.	
"		noon	Batt. extended its front 250 yds. Relieved on night of 13th R.B. and 1st K.R.R.C. or K.R.R. Reinforcements Casualties 2 Officers Killed. (2nd Lt. W.S. HUNTER and Lt. H. LEE the latter died of wounds) Wounded 2 Officers 2nd Lt. A. LYTON, 2nd Lt. H. STONE. Missing 3 2nd/Lt. N. TIMPSON, W.F. WELLS-COLE, and T. McCAIN. Other ranks killed 25, wounded 54, the latter all De Coy. Weather during the two days very unfavourable.	unclassified

Felix Davies Evans
Lt Col
O C 2d Lincolns

War Diary
8th Lincolns
Aug 1917

MESSAGES AND SIGNALS.

Army Form C.2121

TO: 63rd Infantry Bde

Sender's Number.	Day of Month.	In reply to Number.	AAA
*R 33	1-		

AFC 2118 for August herewith

From: 8th Lincoln Regt

WAR DIARY
or
INTELLIGENCE SUMMARY.

Army Form C. 2118.

Place	Date	Hour	Summary of Events and Information	Remarks and references to Appendices
TRENCHES	1.8.17		Battalion maintained its position all day. Relieved at night by 13th R.B. and returned to billet area on KEMMEL HILL.	
BAILLEUL	2.8.17		Battalion moved to rest area between DRANOUTRE and BAILLEUL	
	3.8.17		Battalion rested. 2/Lt WHMAJOR evacuated, suffering from gas poisoning.	WR
	4.8.17		Parades under Company arrangements	WR
	5.8.17		Battalion inspected by Brig. Gen. Challoner. C.O. went on leave.	WR
	6.8.17		Parades under Company arrangements. Working Parties 150 men.	WR
	7.8.17		Parades under Company arrangements {3 Officers } OR Reinforcements: 2nd Lt P DRAPER, E.T.CHRISTIE & A.FARRAR.	WR
CHINESE WALL	8.8.17		Battalion moves into new area (N23 E. Sheet 28.S.W.) Transport R.Q.M. & Coy at GODEZONNE FARM.	WR
	9.8.17		Parades under Company arrangements.	WR
"	10.8.17		Parades under Company arrangements. Working party 100 men	WR
	11.8.17		Parades under Company arrangements. Working party 100 men.	WR
	12.8.17		Battalion Church Parade. Working party 100 men	WR
	13.8.17		Parades under Company arrangement Working party 100 men	WR
	14.8.17		Parades under Company arrangement	WR

Army Form C. 2118.

WAR DIARY
or
INTELLIGENCE SUMMARY.
(Erase heading not required.)

Instructions regarding War Diaries and Intelligence Summaries are contained in F. S. Regs., Part II. and the Staff Manual respectively. Title pages will be prepared in manuscript.

Place	Date	Hour	Summary of Events and Information	Remarks and references to Appendices
TRENCHES	15.8.17		Battalion relieved 11th E. Lancs in Left Sector (from FORRET FARM to GROENLINDE CABt)	WR
	16.8.17		H.Q. at DENYS WOOD. Casualties: 1 Officer 2/Lt BOWDEN + 3 O.R.	WR
			Situation quiet. Enemy shelling, particularly at GREEN WOOD. Casualties 34	WR
	17.8.17		Situation quiet. Intermittent shelling. Casualties 2.	WR
	18.8.17		Situation quiet. Casualties 1.	WR
	19.8.17		Patrol by Lt R H Drake. No Casualties. Heavy bombardment 3-4:30 a.m.	WR
	20.8.17		Patrol by R.Sussex Officer with 3 Lincoln men from near The Twins to HOLLEBEKE. Patrol by 2/Lt BEALES to road junction S.W. of The Twins. Casualties 8.	WR
	21.8.17		Battalion relieved by 6th Bedfds Regt. of D Davies-Evans returned from leave. Casualties nil. Returned to CHINESE WALL	WR
CHINESE WALL	22.8.17		Battalion rests. Major H. MUSSEY went on course	WR
"	23.8.17		Working parties 270 men	WR
"	24.8.17		Working parties whole Battalion	WR
"	25.8.17		Working parties whole Battalion.	WR
WESTOUTRE	26.8.17		Battalion moved to WESTOUTRE. 10th R.Fusiliers took over CHINESE WALL. Working parties continued.	WR
"	27.8.17		Company parades and working parties	WR

WAR DIARY
or
INTELLIGENCE SUMMARY.
(Erase heading not required.)

Army Form C. 2118.

Place	Date	Hour	Summary of Events and Information	Remarks and references to Appendices
WESTOUTRE	28.8.17		Company Parade. Commanding Officer and 3 other Officers reconnoitred new front. Before moving to H Officer 2nd Lt. W.R. GIBSON, H.E. KNEEN, A.F. MITCHELL, T.H. MOODY and 10 O. Rks	W.R.
BOIS CONFLUENT	29.8.17		Battalion moves to BOIS CONFLUENT	
"	30.8.17		Bn in Support. Working party 190 men	W.R.
"	31.8.17		Bn in Support. Working party 205 men. Commanding Officer reconnoitred line	W.R.

Leslie Davis Gray Lt Col
OC 8 Aux'

Vol 24 War Diary
J H Luerton
Sept 1917

Army Form C. 2118.

WAR DIARY
or
INTELLIGENCE SUMMARY.

(Erase heading not required.)

Instructions regarding War Diaries and Intelligence Summaries are contained in F.S. Regs. Part II. and the Staff Manual respectively. Title pages will be prepared in manuscript.

Place	Date	Hour	Summary of Events and Information	Remarks and references to Appendices
BOIS CONFLUENT	1.9.17		Working party 20 men.	
TRENCHES	2.9.17		Batt. relieved 4th Middlesex in HOLLEBEKE sector. C Coy part of A in line. Balance of A, B & D in WHITE CHATEAU. HQ at Bow. Casualties nil	WR
"	3.9.17		White Chateau shelled. Quiet on Front. Work improving line & clearing out dug outs. Casualties nil.	WR
"	4.9.17		Support and WHITE CHATEAU area shelled. No Casualties. Work continued	WR
"	5.9.17		Intermittent shelling. Patrol under 2nd Lt MENTEITH. M.E. encountered enemy. No casualties	WR
"	6.9.17		Intermittent shelling. Work continued. No casualties	WR
ROSSIGNOL WOOD	7.9.17		Battalion relieved by 13th R.F. and returned to ROSSIGNOL WOOD. No casualties	WR
"	8.9.17		Battalion rested.	WR
"	9.9.17		Working parties 150 men. Part of Battn had batt. Church parade. Visit by Brigadier General Chateau B20	WR
BERTHEN	10.9.17		Battalion moved to R24.c.6.2. near BERTHEN. Working party 150 men	WR
"	11.9.17		Working party 150 men. Reinforcements 1 officer 2nd Lt L. CHAMP.	WR
"	12.9.17		Working party 100 men. Reinforcements 4 O.R. A Company fired on range	WR
"	"		Conference of Commanding officers at Bde H.Q.	WR

J W Hugh Capt for OC
Coy 8 Yorks

Army Form C. 2118.

WAR DIARY
or
INTELLIGENCE SUMMARY.
(Erase heading not required.)

Instructions regarding War Diaries and Intelligence Summaries are contained in F. S. Regs., Part II. and the Staff Manual respectively. Title pages will be prepared in manuscript.

Place	Date	Hour	Summary of Events and Information	Remarks and references to Appendices
BERTHEN	13.9.17		Specialist & Company Training. Working party 150 men. Conference of Commanding Officers at Bde HQ.	WR
	14.9.17		Specialist Training.	
	15.9.17		Specialist training in morning.	
	16.9.17		Church Parade. Batt. Drill. Half Holiday.	
	17.9.17		Company & Specialist Training. Conference of Commanding Officers at Bde HQ.	
	18.9.17			
	18.9.17		Tactical Scheme by Bn. in morning. Sports in afternoon.	WR
KEMMEL	19.9.17		Battalion moved to camp at No. 20. Area.	WR
	20.9.17		Parades with Company arrangements.	WR
Nr KOKEREELE	21.9.17		Battalion moved back to OCO billets near BERTHEN. Requirements 1 Officer & 13 O.R.M.	WR
			+ 1 O.R.	
	22.9.17		Parades with Company arrangements. Conference of Commanding Officers at Bde HQ. Football.	WR
	23.9.17		Church Parade.	WR
	24.9.17		Specialist Training with Company arrangements. C Coy fired average Requirement.	
			5 other ranks (=Dh)	

Lt Col M. Murphy
for Lt Col
Cdg. 8. Lincolns

WAR DIARY
or
INTELLIGENCE SUMMARY.

(Erase heading not required.)

Army Form C. 2118.

Place	Date	Hour	Summary of Events and Information	Remarks and references to Appendices
Mt KOKEREELE	25.9.17		Btn Tactical Scheme. 2 platoons C & 2 platoons D Company. Remainder Company having Horse Shows in afternoon.	
	26.9.17		Parades under Company arrangements	
SHREWSBURY FOREST	27.9.17		Batt moved into support in Shrewsbury Forest tents relieving 16th R.B. Reinforcements 5 O.R.	WK WK 6ppts
	28.9.17		Continued shelling. S.O.S. sent up front line: m.r. 27/58, followed by heavy bombardment. Rim. Brown +1 man wounded	bombardment 8ppts
	29.9.17		Continued shelling. S.O.S. sent up in front line: mr. 28/79 followed by heavy bombardment. 1 O.R. killed, 1 O.R. wounded	8ppts
	30.9.17		Continued shelling. S.O.S. sent up in front line: 5 a.m., 6 a.m. and 6.20 a.m. followed by heavy bombardment as before.	8ppts

L.M.[signature]
Lt Col.
O.C. 8. Lincolns

63/37

2/ War Diary
8th Lincoln Regt
Oct 1917

To
63rd Infantry Brigade

Herewith war
Diary for October
1917

EJAChristie
Lieut & Adjt
8 Lincolnshire Regt

1/11/17

37th Division
Passed to you please

[signature]
Major
Brigade Major
63rd Inf Bde
2/11/17

WAR DIARY
or
INTELLIGENCE SUMMARY.

Army Form C. 2118.

Place	Date	Hour	Summary of Events and Information	Remarks and references to Appendices
Trenches	1.10.17		Batt: relieved 4th Middlesex in front line. H.Q. at HET PAPOTE Fm. with 8th S.L.I.	W.R.
	2.10.17		Batt in trenches. Work undertaken:- Establishment of dumps at Bn & Coy HQ.	W.R.
	3.10.17		Continuous shelling. 2 companies 14th Welsh sent up to front line, & occupied support trenches with C. Coy.	
	[4.10.17]			
	4.10.17		Battalion attacked at 6 a.m. Attack unsuccessful. Casualties heavy. Capt R G Codmin, M/Sergt, 2/Lt Farran Horsley Killed; 2/Lt Rotillions & others wounded. Capt R.G. 45 M.or occupied front line with remnants of A, B, & D Companies. Disposition for the attack were as follows: D Coy on left, B Centre, D right, Somewhat in right, 111th Bde (KRRs) on left. Attack on left carried out by 10th KRRs. Result: D Coy reached + apparently crossed road on left, but had to retire. A Coy did not reach road. Enemy in great force at JUTE COTTS, BERRY COTTS + HAMP FARM had attack with heavy Machine gun fire + bombs. Our barrage very poor. In the Evening 2 Companies 10th YORK + LANCS REGT Went up to reinforce. Orders issued for attack and capture of junction in Reinforcements 2.D.R. front line. TOWER TRENCH. North of JUTE	
	5.10.17		Attack on TOWER TRENCH not being possible, posts were advanced North of JUTE COTTS to within 50 yards of German line.	W.R.

WAR DIARY
or
INTELLIGENCE SUMMARY.
(Erase heading not required.)

Army Form C. 2118.

Place	Date	Hour	Summary of Events and Information	Remarks and references to Appendices
IN TRENCHES	6.10.17		Battalion relieved by 1/5 Bedford Regt and returned to their Camp at LITTLE KEMMEL. Total casualties for the tour: 184 O.R. Killed Capt R.G. CORDINER M.C., 2/Lt R.H. WESTOBY, 2nd Lt W.R. GIBSON. Missing 2/Lt	W.R.
AT FORGE			Missing (third) killed 2/Lt R.H. WESTOBY, 2nd Lt W.R. GIBSON. Missing 2/Lt P.H.T. ROBILLIARD. Wounded Lt E.H. DUKES, 2/Lt HEKNEEN.	W.R.
KEMMEL	7.10.17		Battalion rested. Reinforcements 2 O.R. Church Parade.	W.R.
	8.10.17		Training commenced. Conference of Commanding Officers at Bde H.Q. General Plumer was present. Reinforcements 7 O.R.	W.R.
	9.10.17		Training continued. Reinforcements 52 O.R.	W.R.
TREMECRES	10.10.17		Lt/Col. D. DAVIES-EVANS handed over to Major Hon. R.T. ST JOHN and proceeded England. Battalion went into the line at th TOWER HAMLETS Sector, taking over from 1/5 L'N Lanc Regt. Heavily shelled on way up. Many casualties; however very difficult going to wade. Reinforcements 3 O.R.	W.R.
	11.10.17		Quiet in line. Hun shelling in Support and back areas. 2/Lt MULVECK killed at 4 a.m.	W.R.
	12.10.17		Visit by Brig. Gen. Bge F. Bois Grae 659 B.Lt. Quiet day on front line; continued shelling in back.	W.R.
	13.10.17		Quiet day. Usual shelling.	W.R.

WAR DIARY
or
INTELLIGENCE SUMMARY.

Army Form C. 2118.

Place	Date	Hour	Summary of Events and Information	Remarks and references to Appendices
TRENCHES	14.10.17		Day quiet. Visit by GOC 39th Bde. SOS sent up by Somersets on right at 11pm. Artillery continued active for about 3/4 hour. Reinforcements 1 Officer 2/Lt C.G.H. HAMILTON and 2 O.R.	M.R.
	15.10.17		Relieved by 10th HANTS on left and 12th SUSSEX on right. Returned in buses to STAFFORD CAMP at Mt KOKEREELE. Total casualties for tour 43 O.R., 1 Officer 2/Lt D. MULVICK. Battn. rests.	M.R. M.R.
	16.10.17			M.R.
	17.10.17		Conference of Coy. Officers at Bde H.Q. Bn rests. Light parades. Reinforcements 3 Officers, 2/Lts E.T. OWEN, P.H. Paton, J.H. GRAY.	M.R.
	18.10.17		Reinforcements 1 Officer, 2/Lt T.R. WILLCOCKSON. 4 O.R.	M.R.
	19.10.17		Battalion training continued. Reinforcements. 12½ O.R.	M.R.
	20.10.17		Battalion training continued. Officers Football.	M.R.
Mt MERRIS.	21.10.17		Battalion moved to STRAZEELE area, with Bn H.Q. at MERRIS.	M.R.
	22.10.17		Training commenced. Reinforcements 9 Officers, 2/Lts F. MILLS, C. LOWE, H. LOCKYEAR, F.L. WILLETT, F.P. JONES, F. BROWN, W.R. BOUSFIELD, H. SMALLEY, J.S. PLANT and 2 O.R.	M.R.

WAR DIARY
or
INTELLIGENCE SUMMARY.

Army Form C. 2118.

Place	Date	Hour	Summary of Events and Information	Remarks and references to Appendices
MERRIS	23.10.17		Battalion Training continued	
	24.10.17		Training continued. 2/Lt M.STUART-MENTETH left for Third Corps. Reinforcements 20 O.R. Concert in evening.	U.K.
	25.10.17		Battalion Training continued.	U.K
	26.10.17		Training continued. Reinforcements 1 Officer 2nd Lt T. NAYLOR + 4 O.R.	U.K
	27.10.17		Training in morning. Football in afternoon. 2nd Lt LOCKYEAR left	U.K
	28.10.17		Battalion + proceed to 6th LINCOLNS. Church parade. Marching Order inspection by Comdg Officer. Football.	U.K.
	29.10.17		4 Officers + 183 O.R. load with 8th S.L.I. (30 Officers + 833 OR) + 10th Lt. (16 Officers 500 OR) to form working party at St JEAN. 8th S.L.I. details under 8th LINCOLNSHIRE Hd. Lt CHAMP and 2nd Lt DORN proceeded to join	
	30.10.17		Training continued. Supper a range.	Nil U.R
	31.10.17		11th Batt ESSEX Regt. Battalion Training continued	

N.H. Whittell
Lt Col Comdg Bn

"A" Form
MESSAGES AND SIGNALS.

Army Form C. 2121
(in pads of 100).

TO	63rd Infantry Bde.	
Sender's Number.	Day of Month.	In reply to Number.	AAA
R.T. x	2		

Herewith War Diary for November.

From: 8th Lincoln Regt

(Z) M Renwick Capt & Adjt

WAR DIARY
or
INTELLIGENCE SUMMARY
(Erase heading not required.)

Army Form C. 2118.

8 Kings Rgt Vol 26

Place	Date	Hour	Summary of Events and Information	Remarks and references to Appendices
MERRIS	1/11/17		Officers and others at Mont des Cats for course demonstration. Reinforcements on leave. Reinforcements 1 O.R.	BPO BPO
	2/11/17		Training continued. Reinforcements 3 O.R.	BPO
	3/11/17		Rapid wiring practiced 2 i/c - Lt Hartley and i/c 2 O.R. Reinft. Football afternoon v other Bn.	BPO BPO
	4/11/17		Church parade. Cross country run by whole Bn.	BPO
	5/11/17		Training continued. Bde Yukon pack Compn. Bn team selected to compete in Divl Compn. 1 Officer reinforcement Major R.P. Phelps. 1 O.R. reinforcement. Concert in evening.	BPO BPO
	6/11/17.		4 Officers and 183 O.R. returned from leave. Bn team tied with 63rd T.M. By. for first place in Div. Yukon Pack competition. Officers in tactical scheme under G.O.C. & Rev: range.	BPO BPO BPO BPO
	7/11/17		Training continued. Concert in evening. 11 O.R. Reinforcements	BPO
	8/11/17		Battn on range and gas drill. Football v afternoon.	7 gal
DRANOUTRE	9/11/17		Battalion moved to LURGAN LINES for hyper Bde HQ at Locre	7 gal, 7 gal
Bois CARRÉ	10/11/17		Battalion moved to BOIS CARRÉ CAMP. Bgde at KEMMEL	7 gal

Army Form C. 2118.

WAR DIARY
or
INTELLIGENCE SUMMARY.
(Erase heading not required.)

Instructions regarding War Diaries and Intelligence Summaries are contained in F. S. Regs., Part II. and the Staff Manual respectively. Title pages will be prepared in manuscript.

Place	Date	Hour	Summary of Events and Information	Remarks and references to Appendices
BOIS CARRÉ	11/11/17		2 Officers and 100 OR on working parties. Remainder fatigues round area. Remainder fatigue on Camp. Plus	See Apx
	12/11/17		2 Officers and 100 OR on working parties. Remainder on Camp	See Apx
			fatigues and salvage. 1 Officer and 50 OR night working party. 12/13's	See Apx
			Reinforcement 1 OR. Football Batln.	See Apx
	13/11/17		3 Officers and 100 OR on working parties. 1 Officer + 50 OR night party. 13/14's	See Apx
			Work on camp improvement and drainage. Foot drill.	See Apx
	14/11/17		4 Officers and 100 OR working parties. Foot drill. Drainage 1 Officer 150 OR on	See Apx
			night working party. 14th/15	See Apx
	15/11/17		Foot drill. 4 Officer + 100 OR on working parties. Salvage made on Camp. 2 Officers	See Apx
			+ 75 OR on night working party. 15th/16th	See Apx
	16/11/17		4 Officers + 115 OR on working parties. 2 Officers + 50 OR on night working party. 16/17's. Work Apx	See Apx
			on salvage and camp roads.	See Apx
LA CLYTTE	17/11/17		Battn moved to MURRUM BIDGEE CAMP. Battn H.Q. LA CLYTTE. 4 Officers and 125 OR.	See Apx
			on working parties	See Apx
	18/11/17		Church Parade. Pr. notes	See Apx
	19/11/17		Training Commenced. Inspection Co. in full marching order. Baths.	See Apx
			Working parties in Camp. 1 Officer reinforcement. 2/Lt R.H. WOOD. Football	See Apx
			in afternoon	See Apx

WAR DIARY
or
INTELLIGENCE SUMMARY.

Army Form C. 2118.

Place	Date	Hour	Summary of Events and Information	Remarks and references to Appendices
LA CLYTTE	20/11/17		Training continued, work on salvage & improving Camp, Football platoon	8/pal.
	21/11/17		Training and work on camp continued. B + C Coys on range. Battn Football 40 R Preliminaries.	8/pal.
	22/11/17		Training on trenches A & D Coys on range. Football	8/pal.
	23/11/17		Training continued. Football in afternoon. Football	8/pal.
	24/11/17		Training continued. Footballs were during day.	8/pal.
			Bn. relieved 10th R. Irish on front line. H.Q. Post.	8/pal.
TRENCHES	25/11/17		Quiet day. work on support trenches. Wiring in front line.	M.R.
"	26/11/17		All quiet. Work on line continued. to front and support lines.	M.R.
"	27/11/17		Occasional enemy shelling & particularly on No 7 Post. no casualties.	M.R.
"	28/11/17		New post established by Vth on canal bank opposite No 7 Post. Casualties 1 wounded	M.R.
"	29/11/17		New post of Vth taken over by this battalion, line re-grouped in 3 groups ie	M.R.
"	30/11/17		Church Group, Wood-stad Group, Canal Group. New wiring scheme by groups commenced.	M.R.

1. XII – 17

A.J.L. Johnston Lt Col
8th Lincolnshire Reg.

WAR DIARY
or
INTELLIGENCE SUMMARY.

Place	Date	Hour	Summary of Events and Information	Remarks and references to Appendices
TRENCHES	1.12.17		Situation Quiet. Wiring parties continues.	WR
"	2.12.17		Heavy shells intermittently from 4-6 pm from OAK DUMP to B.HQ. Casualties 1 O.R.	WR
"	3.12.17		Quiet day. Casualties 1. Wiring continues	WR
"	4.12.17		Wiring on shell hole and front line carried on. Casualties 2 wounded.	WR
SPOIL BANK	5.12.17		Battalion relieved by 11th Regt Wounded. Heavy shelling of track during relief between front line and OAK DUMP. Casualties 1 killed 1 wounded.	WR
"	6.12.17		Working Parties	WR
"	7.12.17		Working parties + baths	WR
"	8.12.17		Working parties + baths	WR
"	9.12.17		Working parties + baths. Reinforcement	WR
"	10.12.17		Working parties. Visit from Pongelie. Reinforcements 72 O.R.	WR
"	11.12.17		Working parties	WR
"	12.12.17		Working parties. Casualties 2 O.R. wounded.	WR
MURRUMBIDGEE	13.12.17		Working Parties. Battalion moved to MURRUMBIDGEE CAMP	WR
"	14.12.17		Working parties continued	WR
"	15.12.17		Working parties "	WR

WAR DIARY or INTELLIGENCE SUMMARY

Army Form C. 2118.

Place	Date	Hour	Summary of Events and Information	Remarks and references to Appendices
NIEURKAPPELLE	16.12.17		Church Parade. Btl Inspection Staff.	WR
	17.12.17		Training Commenced. Reinforcements 2 Officers 2nd Lts F.L. GOOSEMAN and F.T. INGHAM with	WR
	18.12.17		Training in progress. At Bleyon Range. Reinforcements 48 O.R.	WR
	19.12.17		Battalion having exhms. Football match in afternoon.	WR
	20.12.17		Battalion Christmas Dinner. In work. Reinforcements 32 O.R.	WR
TRENCHES	21.12.17		Battalion took over left sector from 13th R.B.) Preeing & shelling Stow. A Coy on left Front, C on right, B in Support in THE GLEN, D at CORNER HOUSE in Reserve. Two patrols. No casualties.	WR
	22.12.17		Wiring Commenced in front of posts. Cook House installed in newly Salved Bug out. Casualties 1 O.R. wounded.	WR
	23.12.17		Wiring Continued. Casualties 1 killed 1 wounded.	WR
	24.12.17		Enemy Shelling intermittently from 4 to 8pm. Casualties 1 wounded.	WR
	25.12.17		Quiet day. Inter Company Relief, B Coy took over left, D Coy Right, A Coy Support in THE GLEN, C Coy at CORNER HOUSE in Reserve. Relief took place during daylight on our front. Lewis guns fired, no results have not been seen.	WR
	26.12.17		Casualties 2 wounded.	WR

Army Form C. 2118.

WAR DIARY
or
INTELLIGENCE SUMMARY.
(Erase heading not required.)

Instructions regarding War Diaries and Intelligence Summaries are contained in F. S. Regs., Part II. and the Staff Manual respectively. Title pages will be prepared in manuscript.

Place	Date	Hour	Summary of Events and Information	Remarks and references to Appendices
TRENCHES.	26.12.17		HEAVY gas shelling of back areas, including main Gas shells. No damage to front line (battalion.) Casualties 2 wounded.	WR
	27.12.17		Quiet day. Some shelling by heavy shells on Trench Mortars & Shell hole line Casualties 2 wounded (sniper) while wiring in front of posts.)	WR
	28.12.17		Wiring continued actively on front. The whole light through.	WR WR
TOURNAI Camp	29.12.17		1 Battalion relieved by 11th Royal Warwick Regt.) and retired to TOURNAI CAMP. Working parties. Reinforcements 32 O.R. Besides 2 Officers, Lts R. HARTLEY and R.R. WILLCOCKSON. Cross-posted to 2nd Battalion Lincolnshire Regt.	WR
	30.12.17			WR
	31.12.17		Working parties.	WR

R J S John Lt Col
Cdg 8th Lincolnshire Regt

63rd Brigade.
37th Division.

8th BATTALION

THE LINCOLN REGIMENT.

JANUARY 1918

WAR DIARY
or
INTELLIGENCE SUMMARY.
(Erase heading not required.)

Army Form C. 2118.

37/43

8 Wagga
8 Amworth Ry/

Vol 28

Place	Date	Hour	Summary of Events and Information	Remarks and references to Appendices
TOURNAI CAMP.	1.1.18		Battalion on working parties in forward area.	WR
"	2.1.18		Battalion on working parties	WR
"	3.1.18		Battalion on working parties	WR
"	4.1.18		Battalion on working parties. Reinforcement. 1.O.R.	WR
MURRUMBIDGEE	5.1.18		Battalion moves to MURRUMBIDGEE Camp. Working parties continue	WR
"	6.1.18		Battalion on working parties. Church Parade 7.15pm	WR
"	7.1.18		Majority of Bn on working parties. Parades under Coy arrangements.	WR
"	8.1.18		Battalion paraded in morning under Company arrangements. Reinforcement 4.O.R.	WR
"	9.1.18		Battalion paraded under Company arrangements. Divisional RoadCoy + Div Employment Coy men returned to Battalion. Reinforcement 1.O.R. (Div Emp Coy)	WR
"	10.1.18		Battalion wiring party. (Brigade Scheme) working on front line.	WR
MIC MAC Camp	11.1.18		Battalion moved to MIC MAC Camp. (H.31.b.0.6.) GOC 37S Bn visits Camp	WR
"	12.1.18		Working party in forward area 110 other ranks. Remainder works on improvements to Camp.	WR
"	13.1.18		Working party 95 other ranks. Remainder worked on improvements to Camp.	WR
"	14.1.18			WR

2353 Wt. W2514/1454 700,000 5/15 D. D. & L. A.D.S.S. Forms/C. 2118.

Army Form C. 2118.

WAR DIARY
or
INTELLIGENCE SUMMARY.
(Erase heading not required.)

Place	Date	Hour	Summary of Events and Information	Remarks and references to Appendices
Mic Mac Camp	14.1.18		Working parties cancelled. A&B Coy under Coy arrangements. C&D on Camp fatigue	WR
"	15.1.18		A&B Coys working party. C&D Coys on Camp fatigue.	WR
"	16.1.18		150 men on working parties. Remainder on Camp fatigue	WR
"	17.1.18		210 men on working party. Remainder on Camp fatigue	WR
"	18.1.18		220 men on working party. Remainder on Camp fatigue	WR
"	19.1.18		210 men on working party. Remainder on Camp fatigue	WR
"	20.1.18		180 men on working party. Transport moved to STRAZEELE. Church Parade.	WR
WALLON-CAPPEL	21.1.18		Battalion moved by train to WALLON-CAPPEL.	WR
"	22.1.18		Battalion rests. Reinforcement 26 O.R.	WR
"	23.1.18		Parades under Company arrangements	WR
"	24.1.18		Battalion route march. Inspection by Commanding Officer. Reinforcement 526 O.R.	WR
"	25.1.18		Parades under Company arrangements.	WR
"	26.1.18		Preparation for G.O.C's inspection under Company arrangements.	WR
"	27.1.18		Battalion paraded in marching order for inspection by Commanding Officer & followed by Church Parade	WR
"	28.1.18		Battalion inspected by Major General H.B. Williams CB DSO. Company Drill &c.	WR

Army Form C. 2118.

WAR DIARY
or
INTELLIGENCE SUMMARY.
(Erase heading not required.)

Place	Date	Hour	Summary of Events and Information	Remarks and references to Appendices
WALLON-CAPPEL	28.1.18		Continued. 2/Col. Hon R.T. St John went to F.A. Major R.M Phelps assumed command of the Battalion.	WR
	29.1.18		A&B Coy fired on range at C Coy under Coy arrangements.	WR
	30.1.18		Route step under Company arrangements. Reinforcement 31 O.R.	WR
	31.1.18		Preparation for tactical scheme on 1st Feb. B&C Coys on range. A&D under Coy arrangements. A&D Company Lewis Gunners on range.	WR

R.M Phelps Major.

63rd Brigade.
37th Division.

8th BATTALION

THE LINCOLN REGIMENT.

FEBRUARY 1 9 1 8

WAR DIARY
or
INTELLIGENCE SUMMARY.
(Erase heading not required.)

Army Form C. 2118.

Vol 29

Place	Date	Hour	Summary of Events and Information	Remarks and references to Appendices
WALLON CAPPEL	15.2.18		Marched to STRAZEELE	W.R.
FORESTERS CAMP	14.2.18		Battalion moved to FORESTERS CAMP.	W.R.
TRENCHES	15.2.18		Battalion relieved 7th D.C.L.I. in the TOWER HAMLETS Sector. Dispositions, C Coy left front (valley) MENIN ROAD, A Coy right. B in Support E & D Support HA.	W.R.
			Details moved to CHIPPEWA CAMP.	W.R.
"	16.2.18		Details moved to ALBERTA CAMP.	W.R.
"	17.2.18		Situation quiet. Casualties 1 O.R. killed	W.R.
"	18.2.18		Casualties 2 O.R. wounded.	W.R.
"	19.2.18		Situation quiet.	W.R.
"	20.2.18		Situation quiet.	W.R.
"	21.2.18		Battalion relieved by 1st Essex Regt. and retired to SCOTTISH WOOD. Reinforcement 1 O.R.	W.R.
			Casualties 2 O.R. killed	W.R.
SCOTTISH WOOD	22.2.18		Battalion bathed. 7 O.R. went to Bde. as working party. Reinforcements 1 Officer	W.R.
			Capt. H.P. ROBINSON. (10th Y & L. Regt.)	W.R.
CANADA TUNNELS	23.2.18		Battalion relieved 4th Mx Regt. in CANADA TUNNELS. Details went to MASELAQUET CAMP. Battalion disposed as follows:- HQ & B Coy in tunnels CANADA TUNNELS.	W.R.

Army Form C. 2118.

WAR DIARY
or
INTELLIGENCE SUMMARY.
(Erase heading not required.)

Instructions regarding War Diaries and Intelligence Summaries are contained in F. S. Regs., Part II. and the Staff Manual respectively. Title pages will be prepared in manuscript.

Place	Date	Hour	Summary of Events and Information	Remarks and references to Appendices
CANADA TUNNELS	23.9.18		C Coy in ILIAD TRENCH, D Coy in HEDGE STREET TUNNELS, A Coy in Mt SORREL	WR hr
	24.9.18		Working parties.	
TRENCHES	25.9.18		Battalion relieves 4th Mx Regt in front line (TOWER HAMLETS - DUMBARTON WOOD Sector) disposition B Coy left, C Centre D right, A in Suppt. Casualties 10 OR wounded	WR WR
	26.9.18		Quiet day no casualties. Reinforcement 20 OR.	WR
	27.9.18		Practice barrage by our artillery at dawn. Some retaliation shortly after midday	WR
	28.9.18		Intermittent shelling. Reinforcements. Lt Col W WEBB-BOWEN and Captain H5 HEPPER	WR

J H Phelps Major
to his column hrs ref.

63rd Brigade.
37th Division.

8th BATTALION

THE LINCOLN REGIMENT.

MARCH 1918

Army Form C. 2118.

WAR DIARY
or
INTELLIGENCE SUMMARY.
(Erase heading not required.)

Place	Date	Hour	Summary of Events and Information	Remarks and references to Appendices
SCOTTISH WOOD CAMP	1-3-18		Bn. relieved by 8th Somersets L.I. in the line & returned to SCOTTISH WOOD. DETAILS came from MALPLAQUET CAMP	
	2.3.18		Battalion bathed. Working parties	
	3.3.18		Working parties. Bns. in camp. Bathing. U/Sgt. Scot. Programme (Sunday Services)	
	4.3.18		Offg. Officers inspected Latrines, A.R.P. Coys. Working parties. Bns. in camp. 10 OR wounded Cpl.	
	5.3.18		B.O. Coys. hilding parties. Bns. in camp	
	6.3.18		" " " " " 2.1.O.R. reinforcements	
	7.3.18		" inspected Transport. Wkg. parties. Bn. in camp. Captain H.E. HEFFER took up appt of	
	8.3.18		" Nothing. Wkg. parties. Bn. in camp. Adjutant vice Captain M.G. ROWCROFT. Ypres.	
Trenches	9.3.18		" Bn. relieved in "Middlesex" Rgt. on line (TOWER HAMLETS – DUMBARTON WOOD line) Ypres. Details in SCOTTISH WOOD CAMP Ypres.	
			Day quiet. B Centre A Right C Support. 1 O.R. killed 1 O.R. shell shocked	
	10.3.18		Situation quiet. 3 O.R. wounded.	
	11.3.18		Situation quiet. 4 O.R. wounded	
	12.3.18		Intermittent shelling. 1 O.R. killed 1 O.R. died of wounds 10 O.R. wounded	
	13.3.18		Heavy shelling on trench areas. T.M. activ against right Coy. 2 OR wounded Ypres	
	14.3.18		Intermittent shelling of front support lines + B.HQ. 6 an killed 10 OR wounded Ypres	

WAR DIARY or INTELLIGENCE SUMMARY

Army Form C. 2118.

Place	Date	Hour	Summary of Events and Information	Remarks and references to Appendices
Trenches	15.3.18		Bn. retaliated by Arty + Brigade Commanders. Heavy barrage on front + support lines, attempted raid on our right Coy. center off. Bn. relieved by 8 Somerset L.I. + proceeded to CANADA TUNNELS. B. HQ CANADA TUNNELS. A Cy HEDGE ST TUNNELS, B Cy CANADA TUNNELS. D Cy. ILIAD TRENCH and S.P. 1 + 2. C. Cy remained in line in support. 10 O.R. killed 1 O.R. wounded.	Appx
CANADA TUNNELS	16.3.18		Bn. in support. Intermittent shelling on back areas 1 O.R. killed 1 O.R. wounded	Appx
	17.3.18		Intermittent shelling. Casualties nil	Appx
	18.3.18		B Cy. relieved C Cy. as support in line. C Cy CANADA TUNNELS. Heavy intermittent shelling back areas 1 O.R. wounded.	Appx
	19.3.18		Situation quiet. Casualties nil. 21 O.R. reinforcements.	Appx
	20.3.18		" " Casualties 2 O.R. wounded to duty.	Appx
	21.3.18		Heavy gas shelling early morning. Bn. relieved by E Somerset L.I. + Bn. proceeded to SCOTTISH WOOD CAMP. Casualties nil.	Appx
SCOTTISH WOOD CAMP	22.3.18		Bn. cleaned up + foot filled. Working parties.	Appx
	23.3.18		Working parties. Bath at camp. Cy officer inspected B + D Coys. 23 O.R. reinforcements	Appx

WAR DIARY or INTELLIGENCE SUMMARY

Army Form C. 2118.

Place	Date	Hour	Summary of Events and Information	Remarks and references to Appendices
SCOTTISH WOOD CAMP.	24.3.18		Working parties. Work in camp. NCO's instruction. Church parade.	Eph.
TRENCHES	25.3.18		Working parties. Got ruffing. Coy officers inspected A & B Coy working parties. Bttn on Camp Bn. relieved 3rd Aus. Inf. Bn. in front line. BASSEVILLEBEEK - NORTH FARM Sector. C Coy on right. A Coy on left, B Coy, plus 1 section of D Coy, in support. Remainder of D Coy in reserve. Rotario in SCOTTISH WOOD CAMP.	Eph. Eph. Eph. Eph. Eph. Eph. Eph.
	26.3.18		Situation Quiet. 2 OR wounded. Reinforcements 12. OR.	Eph.
	27.3.18		Some shelling of front line. Bn. was relieved in line by XXII Corps Bn. Mounted Troops and proceeded by lorry from KRUISSTRATHOEK CROSS ROADS to FLÊTRE. Details marched from SCOTTISH WOOD 1 OR killed 1 OR wounded	Eph. Eph. Eph. Eph. Eph. Eph.
BILLETS	28.3.18		Battalion rested in billets	Eph.
	29.3.18		Battalion proceeded by train from CAESTRE and joined the IV Corps 3rd Army in the MONDICOURT - PAS area on the morning of 30/3/18.	Eph. Eph. Eph.
	30.3.18		Battalion rested in billets	Eph.
	31.3.18		Battalion proceeded by bunch route to HENU. Were engaged in billets. Commanding officers & party reconnoitres in line	Eph. Eph.

W. Stallan Capt.
for Major
Offg. O.C. 1/8th The Sumberland Regt.

63rd Brigade.
37th Division.

WAR DIARY

8th BATTALION

THE LINCOLN REGIMENT.

APRIL 1918

WAR DIARY
or
INTELLIGENCE SUMMARY

Army Form 2118.

8 Fusiliers

Place	Date	Hour	Summary of Events and Information	Remarks and references to Appendices
HÉNU TRENCHES S.E. of GOMMECOURT	1/4/18		Bn. took over front line S.W. of GOMMECOURT (ROSIGNOL WOOD to SUNKEN Rd.) from 5th K.O.Y.L.I. D right, A centre, B left, C support. Sn. Quiet. Cas. nil	
"	2/4/18		Sn. quiet. Cas. 1 O.R. killed 2 O.R. wounded. Details + Gommecourt under Bqd.	
"	3/4/18		G GOIGNEUX. Sn. Quiet.	
"	4/4/18		Sn. Quiet. Dispositions to advance for attack. D right, A left, C support, B reserve. 1 O.R. killed 1 O.R. wounded. Major A.T. HITCH joined 2nd Command. Bqd.	
"	5/4/18		Bn. attacked at 5.30 a.m. after hvy bomb. but night on three objectives any - K11 C 8.4 to Cemyin, K11 d 03. 20 to K12 C 60.85, K11 d 09 07 to K12 C 88 47. Tanks unable to advance. Considerable resistance first objective where we took objn. 150 prisoners taken or wounded to take 90. Position captured by 5 W.am. Resistance 2nd objective not heavy but considerable m/c gun fire from flanks, Bourbon General on right. Line cleared accepting two strong points, one on final objective on right. Position heavily consolidated by 7.45 a.m. Enemy counter-attacked in locus approaches. ROSIGNOL WOOD at 9 a.m. Enemy reinforced about mid-day. We were not in touch with 8° Somersets on left or Bqd.	

WAR DIARY
or
INTELLIGENCE SUMMARY.

Army Form C. 2118

Place	Date	Hour	Summary of Events and Information	Remarks and references to Appendices
S.E. of GOMMECOURT	5/4/18 Contd.		Australians on our right. Our small garrison in Essex Trench gradually driven & Southwards into Essex system. About 1 pm enemy advanced from his strong points on our right and on our left. Being outnumbered shortly of bombs we fought a rear-guard action for over three hours till he withdrew in good order at about 5.30 pm into our original front line. Many casualties inflicted on enemy and all his M/G from DUCK TRENCH were destroyed. 14 enemy a/c from contact aeroplanes were seen from 2.30 pm but were accounted for. Withdrawing foremost waves was established at H.11.C.6.5. under 7th Hamilton who kept enemy until bombed out. Artillery rifle gun barrage excellent. Many casualties very useful. Private Gamble implicated in enemy position. Min behaved splendidly, rifle work heavy. Casualties 2/Lt P.H. PEADON wded. (died of wounds) 2/Lt G.H.L. ASKEY wded (died of wounds) 2/Lt H.E MOODY wounded + missing 2/Lt G. LOWE wounded. 2 O.R. killed 107 OR wounded 62 OR missing.	See See See See See See See See See See See See See See See See
	6/4/18		Bn. relieved by 13th R.Bgde and moved into tunnels - GOMMECOURT WOOD in Brigade reserve. Sit quiet. Details remained at COIGNEUX	See See

2353 Wt W2544/1451 700,000 5/15 D.D.&L. A.D.S.S.-Forms/C. 2118.

WAR DIARY or INTELLIGENCE SUMMARY

Army Form C. 2118.

Place	Date	Hour	Summary of Events and Information	Remarks and references to Appendices
GOMMECOURT WOOD	7/4/18		Sit. Quiet. Bn. rested. Bathed. Reinforcements 25 O.R.	JJW
"	8/4/18		Sit. Quiet. Bathing + further dummy aun	JJW
"	9/4/18		Intermittent shelling of GOMMECOURT WOOD ~ 1 OR killed. 2 OR wounded at night	JJW
S.E. of GOMMECOURT.			Bn. relieved 6th BEDFORDS in front line. K.12.6. 38.20 - L.7.d. 08.98.	JJW
			B Cy on right, D Cy on left, C Cy in support, A Cy in reserve. Sit Quiet	JJW
			Details remained at COIGNEUX	JJW
"	10/4/18		Sit. Quiet. 37th Div Composite Bn. joined from details. Reinft. 52 O.Rs.	JJW
"	11/4/18		Sit. Quiet. Reinforcements. 6 ORs.	JJW
"	12/4/18		Heavy shelling of RETTEMOY FARM aun at night. B. extended to left & took over from 4th Middlesex Regt to L.7.b. 85.15. 8th Somerset L.I. took over from D Cy on right.	JJW
			near of 2nd line dummy N of Lahmer Spinney K.12.L.7	JJW
"	13/4/18		Sit. Quiet. Cas 1 OR killed. 6 OR wounded	JJW
"	14/4/18		Sit. Quiet. Bn. relieved by 4th Middlesex Regt. & went into support in lines N of GOMMECOURT WOOD (E.27.a). Reinforcements. 2/4 F.D. Forge + 20 OR	JJW
H of GOMMECOURT WOOD HENU.	15/4/18		Bn. rested during day. Bathing. At night Bn. relieved by 8th Cheshire Regt + moved into billets at HENU. Transport + rear HQ moved to HENU also. Sit Quiet. 2/4 F.L. WOOLATT + 2 O.R wounded.	JJW

WAR DIARY
or
INTELLIGENCE SUMMARY.

Army Form C. 2118.

Place	Date	Hour	Summary of Events and Information	Remarks and references to Appendices
HENU AUTHIE	16/4/18		Battalion moved into Camp (under canvas) in AUTHIE WOOD. Details 87th from 37th Divl Composite Bn. rejoined Bn. Reinforcements 87 O.R.	87ab ?
	17/4/18		Cleaning up & Coy. inspection. Bn. at 1 hours notice. Reinforcements 2 O.R.	?
	18/4/18		Training. Coys. inspected by Coy Officers. Reinforcements 2/Lt H. BROOKS and 2/Lt J.R. HALL. Crew-posted joint 13th K.R.R.C	? ?
	19/4/18		Training at day. Lewis Gunners (untrained) in range Practice. No 36 Grenade. Reconnaissance of PURPLE LINE by CO + Coy Officers. Reinft.	? ?
	20/4/18		Training at day. Reconnaissance of PURPLE LINE by Coy Officers. Reinfts. 4 O.Rs. Recreational training in afternoon	? ?
	21/4/18		Working party 8 Officers 1 350 O.R. Remainder in Lewis Gun Training Specialist training under specialist officers. Remainder under O.C Coys. Inhaling 1 Gunners in range 37th Divl Trench Mortar and S.O.A Coys. Bathing at AUTHIE. Bn. relieved 2/4 York + Lancs at E 30.5 (N.E. of GOMMECOURT)	? ? ?
	22/4/18		in SUPPORT. Details under S.S.135 remained with 37th Divl Composite Bn. at AUTHIE. Rear H.Q. moved in billets at SOUASTRE. Situation quiet. Casualties nil. Reinforcements 9 O.Rs.	? ? ?

War Diary or Intelligence Summary

Army Form C. 2118.

Place	Date	Hour	Summary of Events and Information	Remarks and references to Appendices
Trenches	24/4/18		Quiet day. Casualties nil	
	25/4/18		Enemy shelling. Casualties nil. Reinforcements 2/Lieut A.D. King, 2/Lt F.M. Idmore, 2/Lt D.W. Blunt, 2/Lt L. Knefton, 2/Lt A.D. Mathewman, 2/Lt G.A. Bradley, 2/Lt J. Scoggs, 2/Lt V. Warman, 2/Lt A. Swales, 2/Lt H.J. Mechlin, 2/Lt H.S. Brooks.	2/L
	26/4/18		Quiet day. Casualties nil. One case S.I.W.	
	27/4/18		Intermittent shelling. Batt relieved 4 Welsh Regt in the line. S.J. BUCADOY C Coy left, D Coy right. A Support Coy in B Ravine. Casualties 2 O.Rs killed, 3 O.Rs wounded. 1 O.R. wounded to duty. Reinforcements Lieut J.M. Allbones, 2/Lt L. McBean, 2/Lt A.N. Beattie, 5 O.Rs.	
	28/4/18		Quiet day. Casualties nil.	
	29/4/18		Intermittent shelling. Cas. 2/Lt J.R. Bonafield and 2 O.Rs wounded. Reinforcement 1 O.R.	
	30/4/18		Quiet day. Cas. 4 O.Rs wounded.	

A. Welch Major for Major
Comg 6 Lincolnshire Regt.

63rd Brigade.
37th Division.

8th BATTALION

THE LINCOLN REGIMENT.

MAY 1918

WAR DIARY
or
INTELLIGENCE SUMMARY.
(Erase heading not required.)

Army Form C. 2118.

Place	Date	Hour	Summary of Events and Information	Remarks and references to Appendices
Humbercamps	1/5/18		Quiet day. Battalion relieved by 13th R.F. and moved back into reserve at ESSART. C Coy HQ. B Coy Centre, A Coy Left, D Coy in support. Casualties 6 o.r. wounded	
	2/5/18		Quiet day. Battalion in reserve 1 o.r. killed	
	3/5/18		Quiet day. Cas. nil. Reinfts. 2 O.Rs.	
	4/5/18		Quiet day. Cas. Nil.	
	5/5/18		Quiet day. Battalion relieved by 8th Somersets L.I. and moved back into VALLEY CAMP SOUASTRE. Bn HQ in SOUASTRE. Casualties nil.	
	6/5/18		Battalion rested. Cleaned up & bathed.	
	7/5/18		Battalion resting. Cleaning up. Wet day. Reinforcement 1 2/Lt Gibbons, 7 O.R.s	
	8/5/18		Commanding Officer inspected the Battalion by Companies. 4 O.R. reinforcements	
	9/5/18		Battalion relieved 13th R.B. in the line at BUCQUOY. A Coy right, B Coy left, C Coy Right Support, D Coy Left support. J. O.R. Reinforcements. Casualties Nil.	

WAR DIARY or INTELLIGENCE SUMMARY

Army Form C. 2118.

Place	Date	Hour	Summary of Events and Information	Remarks and references to Appendices
Trenches	10/5/18		Quiet day. Casualties NIL. Reinforcements 5 O.R.	
	11/5/18		Intermittent shelling. Casualties 5 O.R. wounded. Reinforcements NIL	
	12/5/18		FONQUEVILLERS heavily shelled with gas. Casualties NIL. Reinforcements NIL	
	13/5/18		Quiet day. Casualties 1 O.R. wounded. Reinforcements NIL	
	14/5/18		Quiet day. Casualties NIL. Reinforcements NIL	
	15/5/18		Support trenches heavily shelled. Casualties NIL. Reinforcements 5 O.R.	
	16/5/18		Quiet day. Casualties NIL. Batt. relieved by 2/4th Duke of Wellingtons Regt. Batt. withdrew to BOIS DU WARNIMONT. Casualties 1 O.R. wounded. Reinforcements 6 O.R.	
	17/5/18		Batt. in 4th Army reserve. 2 O.R. Reinforcements NIL	
	18/5/18		Batt. cleaned up. Reinforcements 1 O.R.	
	19/5/18		Batt. batted. Church Parade. 1 Company. Reinforcements	
	20/5/18		A & B Coys on Range. Musketry & Lewis Gunn. C & D Coys on	

WAR DIARY or INTELLIGENCE SUMMARY

Army Form C. 2118.

Place	Date	Hour	Summary of Events and Information	Remarks and references to Appendices
Tuesday				
	21/5/18		General Training. Specialist Training was also carried out. Reinforcements: 1 OFFICER, NZ Rochdale Fwd. A & B Coys Divisional Training CRD Coy Range, Musketry & Lewis Gun. Specialist Training carried out with Reinforcements to S.O.R.	Fwd NZA, NZA NZA, NZA
	22/5/18		Battalion on working party under R.E., digging on PURPLE LINE. Bon Reputation rom from 4 pm to 8 pm.	NZA, NZA, NZA, NZA, NZA
	23/5/18		Lewis Gun & Musketry Training carried out. Gas tuition by Divl Gas Officer. Bon Reputation from 10 am to 11 am. Reinforcements 55 O.R. Casualties NIL	NZA, NZA, NZA, NZA
	24/5/18		Battn relieved 2nd Canterbury N.Z. Regt in trenches in the PURPLE LINE. Casualties NIL Reinforcements NIL	NZA, NZA
	25/5/18		Battn in PURPLE LINE. Battn on digging trenches in PURPLE LINE. 1 hour musketry & Bon Reputation Training carried out. Reinforcements & Casualties NIL	NZA, NZA, NZA

Army Form C. 2118.

WAR DIARY
or
INTELLIGENCE SUMMARY.
(Erase heading not required.)

Instructions regarding War Diaries and Intelligence Summaries are contained in F. S. Regs., Part II. and the Staff Manual respectively. Title pages will be prepared in manuscript.

Place	Date	Hour	Summary of Events and Information	Remarks and references to Appendices
Trenches	26/5/18		Battn in PURPLE LINE. Battn digging trenches under R.E. Reinforcements & Casualties NIL. 1 Lewis gunner out. Box Respirator Training.	7 W.A 3 W.A
	27/5/18		Battn in PURPLE LINE. Battn digging trenches under R.E. 1 Lewis Instructor Training. NIL. Reinforcements & Casualties out.	7 W.A 2 W.A 3 W.A 4 W.A
	28/5/18		Battn in Purple Line. Battn digging trenches under R.E. 1 Lewis Musketry Training. Casualties 5 O.R.	1 W.A 3 W.A
	29/5/18		Battn in Purple Line. Battn digging trenches under R.E. 1 Lewis Musketry Training. Battn Appr. & Rifle demonstration by Officers. Casualties NIL.	7 W.A 2 W.A
	30/5/18		Battn in Purple Zone. Battn digging trenches under 10th R.F. not with us. Battn relieved. Reinforcements 55 O.R. Billets to AUTHIE. Casualties NIL.	7 W.A 7 W.A 2 W.A
	31/5/18		Battn in Billets. Cleaning up & Kit Inspections.	7 W.A 2 W.A

Army Form C. 2118.

WAR DIARY
or
INTELLIGENCE SUMMARY.
(Erase heading not required.)

Place	Date	Hour	Summary of Events and Information	Remarks and references to Appendices
Taurelis	31/5/18 (contd)		Reinforcements Y.O.R. Battalion. Parade at 2 pm 7 a.A. A/R.S.M. Beeton joined Battalion, and took over 1 a.A duties of R.S.M. 7 a.A	

A. Nitch Major
Comdg 8th Lincolnshire Regt.

63rd Brigade.
37th Division.

8th BATTALION

THE LINCOLNSHIRE REGIMENT.

JUNE 1918

WAR DIARY or INTELLIGENCE SUMMARY

Army Form C. 2118.

8 Lincoln Regt.

No 33

Place	Date	Hour	Summary of Events and Information	Remarks and references to Appendices
Trenches	1/6/18		Batta on 'F' Prisoner Escort. General Training carried out. Practice Training in afternoon. Reinforcements	?WA
	2/6/18		NIL	?WA
	3/6/18		Church Parade. Reinforcements 8. O.R.	?WA
			Gas Lecture by Divl Gas Officer. Batta on Ranges 9WA (Musketry & Lewis Gun) Reinforcements 15 ?WA	?WA
			in afternoon. Reinforcements 2. O.R.	?WA
	4/6/18		Batta on Ranges A.R.A. Competition carried out.	?WA
			Transport Competition. Reinforcements NIL.	?WA
	5/6/18		Assembly Parade at 11 a.m. All Training cancelled.	?WA
			Batta entrained at 9.30 p.m. en route to Heilly ?WA	?WA
			in FOUR DRINOY. Reinforcements 2. O.R.	?WA
	6/6/18		Batta arrived in billets at FOUR DRINOY. at 9 a.m ?WA	?WA
			Batta rested reminder of day. Reinforcements NIL.	?WA
	7/6/18		Batta assembled to inspect ammunition em. CO attended	?WA
			conference at Bde H.Q. Reinforcements & Casualties NIL	?WA

Army Form C.2118.

WAR DIARY
or
INTELLIGENCE SUMMARY.
(Erase heading not required.)

Place	Date	Hour	Summary of Events and Information	Remarks and references to Appendices
Tincourt	8/6/18		Reconnoitring party consisting of C.O. 2 Company Commanders & Intelligence Officer proceeded to reconnoitre training area. Training under Company arrangements. Reinforcements & Casualties NIL.	P.W.A
	9/6/18		Church Parade. Lecture at 12 noon at Bde H.Q.R.S.P. Reinforcements & Casualties NIL.	P.W.A
	10/6/18		Battn moved to fields in LOEUILLY by French Motor Buses. Training under Company arrangements. Reinforcements NIL.	P.W.A
	11/6/18		Companies at disposal of Company Commanders. G.O.C.'s parade. Recreational training carried out. Reinforcements.	P.W.A
	12/6/18	12 Noon 5.O.R.	Battalion paraded through Gas Chamber by Companies. Musketry & Lewis Gun training. Bore Retreats. NCO's on range. Reinforcements NIL	P.W.A P.W.A
	13/6/18		Under Bn. Arrangements. Tactical Scheme carried out. Reinforcements 4th Inniskilling 6.	P.W.A P.W.A
	14/6/18		Bde. Reinforcements NIL. Battn relieved 4th Inniskilling in billets at ORESMAUX. Training under Company arrangements. Battn. relieved	P.W.A P.W.A
	15/6/18		at RUMIGNY by ..... in the evening. Reinforcements NIL.	P.W.A P.W.A

13 R 750

Army Form C. 2118.

WAR DIARY
or
INTELLIGENCE SUMMARY.
(Erase heading not required.)

Instructions regarding War Diaries and Intelligence Summaries are contained in F. S. Regs., Part II. and the Staff Manual respectively. Title pages will be prepared in manuscript.

Place	Date	Hour	Summary of Events and Information	Remarks and references to Appendices
Trenches	16/6/18		Church Parade. LIEUT HANSELL proceeded to England to join R.A.F. Reinforcements 1 O.R.	2WA
	17/6/18		Battalion Field Day practice attack formations. Reinforcements NIL.	2WA 2WA 2WA
	18/6/18		Training under Company arrangements. Reinforcements NIL/RM	2WA
	19/6/18		Tactical Training. B Coy on Range A,C & D under Company arrangements. Reinforcements 11 O.R.	2WA 2WA
	20/6/18		Training under Company arrangements. Reinforcements NIL/WA	2WA
	21/6/18		Battalion entrained at PROUZEL and proceeded to COUIN. Reinforcements NIL 2/Lieut FLINT sent to hospital.	2WA 2WA 2WA
	22/6/18		Batt. cleaning up. S.B.R. tests carried out. G.O.C. Conference at Bde H.Q. Reinforcements NIL.	2WA 2WA
	24/6/18		Training under Company arrangements. Batt. party reconnoitre trenches. Reinforcements NIL.	2WA 2WA
	23/6/18		Church Parade. A & B Coys Batt. Reinforcements NIL	2WA
	25/6/18		Batt. relieved 2/4th York & Lancs in trenches at ESSARTS. Reinforcements to CANNETRE NIL	2WA 2WA

Army Form C.2118.

WAR DIARY
or
INTELLIGENCE SUMMARY.
(*Erase heading not required.*)

Instructions regarding War Diaries and Intelligence Summaries are contained in F. S. Regs., Part II. and the Staff Manual respectively. Title pages will be prepared in manuscript.

Place	Date	Hour	Summary of Events and Information	Remarks and references to Appendices
Trenches	26/6/18		Battn in Trenches. Slight shelling. Casualties 1. O.R.	9wA
	27/6/18		" " " " " " Casualties NIL	9wA
	28/6/18		" " " " " " Casualties 3 O.R.	9wA
	29/6/18		" " " " " " Casualties NIL	9wA
	30/6/18		" " " " " " Casualties 3. O.R.	9wA

A. Ffitch.
Lt Col
Comdg 8th Lincolnshire Regt

63rd Brigade.
37th Division.

8th BATTALION

THE LINCOLNSHIRE REGIMENT

JULY 1918

WAR DIARY or INTELLIGENCE SUMMARY

Army Form C. 2118.

8 Lincoln Rgt

Place	Date	Hour	Summary of Events and Information	Remarks and references to Appendices
Trenches	1/7/18		Battn in Support. Artillery active. Battn relieved 4th Bn Middlesex Regt in the Left Sub Sector. "A" Coy Right Front. "C" Coy Left Front. "D" Coy Right Support "B" Coy Left Support. Bn HQ TOR TRENCH. Casualties Nil.	
"	2/7/18		Battalion in line. Heavy shelling of back areas Cas. nil. Reinforcements 1 O.R.	
"	3/7/18		Battn in line. Quiet day. Cas Nil	
"	4/7/18		" " " " A Gas Projector attack carried out against ABLAINZEVELLE at 12.30 a.m. Retaliation with mustard shelling of Front line. Cas 6 O.R. wounded. 1 O.R. S.I.W.	
"	5/7/18		Battn in the line. Back area heavily shelled Cas 1 O.R. S.I.W.	
"	6/7/18		" " " " Left Front Coy shelled with Gas & H.E. Cas Nil.	
"	7/7/18		21 O.R. Gassed	
"	8/7/18		Battn in the line. Quiet day. Battn relieved by the 13th Rifle Brigade Regt and with-drew exception D Coy into billets at SOUASTRE. D Cy Coy proceeded to CHATEAU DE LA HAIE SWITCH. Battn in Reserve Brigade. Cas 2/Lt H.F. MEHEW and 6 O.R. wounded.	
SOUASTRE	8/7/18		Battn in billets. Cleaning up.	
"	9/7/18		" C.O's Inspection A + C Coys. B Coy range + Musketry Party Football Match. Concert.	

Army Form C. 2118.

WAR DIARY
or
INTELLIGENCE SUMMARY.
(Erase heading not required.)

Instructions regarding War Diaries and Intelligence Summaries are contained in F. S. Regs., Part II. and the Staff Manual respectively. Title pages will be prepared in manuscript.

Place	Date	Hour	Summary of Events and Information	Remarks and references to Appendices
Trenches	10/7/18		Battn relieve the 4th Middx Regt in the "Z" A + C Coys BEER TRENCH B Coy Pyrian Wood D Coy Events. Res TB Hardy DSO MC awarded the Victoria Cross. Reinforcements & Casualties NIL.	R/A R/A
	11/7/18		Batt in Trenches. Quiet day Casualties NIL	R/A
	12/7/18		" " intermittent shelling Casualties 2 O.R. wounded	R/A
	13/7/18		" " Battn relieve the 10th Royal Fusiliers in left Subsector "Blog" Right front "D" Coy left front "A" Coy Right support 5 I O R.	R/A R/A
	14/7/18		"C" Coy Left support. Casualties NIL. Reinforcements NIL	R/A R/A
	15/7/18		Battn in trenches Quiet day Casualties & Reinforcements NIL Hostile Battery action Casualties 1 O R. STN.	R/A R/A
	16/7/18		Reinforcements NIL Batt in trenches Intermittent shelling Casualties & reinforcements 48 R/A	R/A
			NIL. Batt relieved by 8th Somerset L I Batt moves over to support A Coy N.B. Rothuney farm R Coy	R/A R/A
	17/7/18		B Coy Gouvecourt Trench C Coy Kits Trench D Coy to Angele Avenue Casualties 2/Lieut NAYLOR	R/A R/A
			wounded Reinforcements 30 O.R.	R/A
	18/7/18		Battn in trenches Intermittent shelling Casualties & Reinforcements	R/A
			NIL	R/A
	19/7/18		Battn in trenches. Quiet day Casualties 1 O.R. killed 1 O.R. wounded. R/A	R/A
	20/7/18		" " Intermittent shelling. Casualties & Reinforcements NIL. R/A	R/A

Army Form C. 2118.

WAR DIARY
or
INTELLIGENCE SUMMARY.
(Erase heading not required.)

Place	Date	Hour	Summary of Events and Information	Remarks and references to Appendices
Trenches	21/7/18		Battn. relieved the 4th Princess Pat's Light Infantry Regt. Battn. HQ Rotenoy Farm. 'A' Coy Right Front. 'C' Coy Left Front. 'B' Coy Reserve. D'y Support. Casualties 10.R. Killed 5 O.R. Wounded. Reinforcements 1 Officer (Lieut. Litterwill Cook) Casualties 10.R. Recruitment.	P.W.A P.W.A P.W.A P.W.A P.W.A
	22/7/18		Battn. in Trenches. Intermittent shelling. Casualties & Reinforcements NIL.	P.W.A
	23/7/18		Battn. in Trenches. Raid repulsed by our 'K' post. Enemy wounded prisoner. Casualties & reinforcements. 1 Officer (Lt. Godfrey) Battn. in Trenches. Hostile artillery active. Casualties 1 O.R. killed. 5 O.R. wounded. Reinforcements NIL.	P.W.A P.W.A P.W.A
	24/7/18			P.W.A
	25/7/18		Battn. in Trenches. Hostile artillery active. Casualties & Reinforcements 1 Officer (Lieut. Proctor). Battn. relieved by 13 Rifle Brigade & returned to SOUASTRE (Valley Camp). Casualties 1.O.R. wounded. Reinforcements 1 Officer Lieut. B. Bamber. 33 O.R. other ranks.	P.W.A P.W.A P.W.A
	26/7/18			P.W.A P.W.A P.W.A
SOUASTRE	27/7/18		Battn. Bathed & cleaned up. Working party of 2 Officers & 100 O.Ranks under 37th Div. Signal Coy.	P.W.A P.W.A
	28/7/18		Companies on range. Divn Gas Training Carried out. Working party of 2 Officers & 100 O.R. under 37 Div Signal Coy. Reinforcements & Casualties NIL. Consent by Rgt Bene. Companies on range. Battalion relieved to find Reinforcements & Casualties in the Bn.	P.W.A P.W.A P.W.A P.W.A
	29/7/18		Z. Trenches near LA BRAYELLE FARM. Reinforcements & Casualties NIL. Capt A.R. Robinson proceeded to join R.A.F.	P.W.A P.W.A

Army Form C. 2118.

WAR DIARY
or
INTELLIGENCE SUMMARY.
(Erase heading not required.)

Instructions regarding War Diaries and Intelligence Summaries are contained in F. S. Regs., Part II. and the Staff Manual respectively. Title pages will be prepared in manuscript.

Place	Date	Hour	Summary of Events and Information	Remarks and references to Appendices
Trenches	30/4/18		Batt. in Trenches. Quiet day. Working parties under R.E. Shelled Sergt Drummer Bilinger Killed. Reinforcements NIL.	SOVASTRE P634 P634 P634 P634 P634.
	31/4/18		Batt. in Trenches. Quiet day. Working Parties under R.E. Reinforcements & Casualties NIL.	

A.T.Hitch. Lieut Col.
Comdg. 8th Battn The Lincolnshire Regt.

In the Field
1/5/18.

63rd Brigade.
37th Division.

8th BATTALION

THE LINCOLNSHIRE REGIMENT.

AUGUST 1918

WAR DIARY
or
INTELLIGENCE SUMMARY.

Army Form C. 2118

8 Suffolk Regt
Vol 35

Place	Date	Hour	Summary of Events and Information	Remarks and references to Appendices
Trenches	1/8/18		Battalion in Trenches. Quiet day. Casualties + reinforcements NIL	Ph1A
	2/8/18		Battalion relieves 1st Essex Regt in Left Sector. Casualties + Reinforcements NIL	Ph1A, 2h A
	3/8/18		Battalion in Trenches. Quiet day. Casualties + Reinforcements NIL	Ph1A
	4/8/18		do do do do	Ph1A
	5/8/18		do do do do	Ph1A
	6/8/18		do do do 2/Lieut MANSELL	Ph1A
	7/8/18		do do do NIL	Ph1A
	8/8/18		do 4 O.R. wounded, 2 O.R. to Hospital	Ph1A
			Battalion relieved by 4th Middlesex Regt and moved into Suffolk Avenue near ESSARTS.	Ph1A
	9/8/18		Battalion in Trenches working parties under R.E. Casualties + reinforcements NIL.	Ph1A
	10/8/18		Battalion in Trenches. Quiet day. Casualties 2 O.R. wounded	Ph1A
	11/8/18		Reinforcements NIL. Battalion in Trenches. Quiet day. Casualties 2 O.R. killed 4 O.R. Reinforcements NIL.	Ph1A
	12/8/18		8 O.R. wounded. Battalion in Trenches. Close Lys Arras on Bucquoy by Special Coy R.E. Casualties 1 O.R. wounded. Reinforcements 2/Lieut WELBY, 2/Lieut BLAKEY.	Ph1A

WAR DIARY
or
INTELLIGENCE SUMMARY

Army Form C. 2118.

Place	Date	Hour	Summary of Events and Information	Remarks and references to Appendices
Trenches	13/8/18		Battalion relieved 8" Somerset L.I. in Right Subsector BUCQUOY. Casualties NIL. Reinforcements NIL.	F.W.A. F.W.A.
	14/8/18		Battalion in trenches. Quiet day. Casualties 1 O.R. wounded. Reinforcements NIL.	F.W.A. F.W.A.
	15/8/18		Battalion in trenches. Patrols active. Reinforcements NIL. Casualties NIL.	F.W.A. F.W.A.
	16/8/18		Battalion in trenches. Raid on CEMETERY by D.Coy. No prisoners. No casualties. Enemy reported to be returning in force of BUCQUOY. Reinforcements NIL.	F.W.A. F.W.A. F.W.A.
	17/8/18		Battalion relieved by 13 K.R.R.C. and withdrew to SOUASTRE. A & C Companies in CHATEAU DE LA HAIE SWITCH. Reinforcements & Casualties NIL	F.W.A. F.W.A.
	18/8/18		Battalion cleaning up. Concerts by the Regimental Band. Reinforcements & Casualties NIL.	F.W.A. F.W.A.
	19/8/18		Battalion Battle Concerts by Regimental Band. In the evening Battalion proceeded to SUPPORT AREA thereunto to PIGEON WOOD. Rear Headquarters moved from SOUASTRE to Transport Lines. Reinforcements & Casualties NIL.	F.W.A. F.W.A. F.W.A. F.W.A.

Army Form C. 2118.

WAR DIARY
or
INTELLIGENCE SUMMARY.

(Erase heading not required.)

Instructions regarding War Diaries and Intelligence Summaries are contained in F.S. Regs, Part II. and the Staff Manual respectively. Title pages will be prepared in manuscript.

Place	Date	Hour	Summary of Events and Information	Remarks and references to Appendices
Trenches	20/8/18		Battalion in support Trenches. Quiet day. Battn. preparing for attack on BUCQUOY. Casualties NIL	N/A N/A
	21/8/18		Battalion took BUCQUOY in conjunction with 8th Somerset L.I. Casualties 3 OR killed 6 OR wounded. All objectives gained. Reinforcements NIL	N/A N/A

Reference Sheet 57D NE Edition 3 d (local) 1/20,000

August 19th.
The Battalion moved to PIGEON WOOD preparatory to the attack.

August 20th.
The Battalion moved forward to positions WEST OF BUCQUOY.
"A" Company F.27.d.10.10 to F.27.d.35.50.
"B" Company in HEDGE TRENCH, F.27.c.50.40 to F.27.c.80.80.
"C" Company BUSH TRENCH, F.27.d.00.00 to F.27.d.20.60.
"D" Company in Sunken Road, F.27.c.60.65 to F.27.c.40.40.
Battalion Headquarters, F.26.a.50.10.
Casualties Nil.

August 21st.
Companies still maintained the same positions with the exception of "A" Company, who moved forward to gardens from F.27.d.50.10 - F.27.d.60.40.
At 4.45 a.m. Battalion moved forward in support to 8th Somerset L.I. "A" Company consolidated a line of posts from L.4.c.05.90 to F.26.c.30.00 "B" Company consolidated a line of posts with 2 Platoons from L.3.a.50.00 to L.3.c.20.40. 1 Platoon at L.5.c.10.90. 1 Platoon in CLIFF TRENCH— L.2.d.25.30 to L.2.d.30.70.
"C" Company in HEDGE TRENCH, F.27.c.70.60 to F.27.c.90.15.
"B" Company, 2 Platoons at L.3.d.70.40. 1 Platoon L.9.a.90.05.
1 Platoon L.9.c.30.90.
Casualties:- 3 other ranks killed - 6 other ranks wounded.
Heavy shelling of Southern edge of BUCQUOY throughout the day.

WAR DIARY
or
INTELLIGENCE SUMMARY.
(Erase heading not required.)

Army Form C.2118.

Place	Date	Hour	Summary of Events and Information	Remarks and references to Appendices
Trenches				Reference Sheet 57c NW Edition 9a Local 1/20,000

August 22nd
Battalion holding the same position.
Battalion moved into the Valley N.E. of ASHAINEVELLE in A.19.d. and A.20.c. taking up the position on the left of the Middlesex Regiment. Battalion Headquarters at A.19.d.70.80.

August 23rd
11 a.m. Battalion moved forward in S. Easterly direction as the left support Battalion to the 111th Brigade (left Brigade attacking ACHIET-LE-GRANDE & BIHUCOURT). 111th Brigade obtained their objective and established a line East of BIHUCOURT.
Battalion established themselves in trenches North of BIHUCOURT.
"A" Company G.11.c.30.80 to G.11.c.50.95.
"B" Company G.11.c.50.95 to G.11.a.75.15.
"C" Company G.11.a.75.15 to G.11.a.85.30.
"D" Company G.11.a.95.05 to G.11.b.20.40.
Battalion Headquarters G.5.d.65.30.
5.30 p.m. Battalion advanced through the outpost line.
"C" Company Left Front - "A" Company Right Front - "D" Company Left Support
"B" Company Right Support.
Battalion pushed forward, reaching general line from G.17.b.90.90 to G.12.c.40.50.
Very heavy Machine Gun Fire was encountered - flanks were in the air.
Battalion was forced to move back and take up their original position.
Casualties ?

August 24th.
At 4.30 a.m. Battalion moved forward, assembling on general lines on the Eastern edge of BIHUCOURT with the object of pushing N.E. of BIEFVILLERS.
At 2 p.m. Battalion moved round South Western edge of BIHUCOURT into the Valley S.E. of BIHUCOURT, assembling there with the object of establishing a line from BIHUCOURT to BIEFVILLERS.
Dispositions:-
"A" Company on Right.   "B" Company Centre
"D" Company on Left   "C" Company in Support.

The 3 Front Companies pushed forward:-
"A" Company. 1 Platoon at G.18.b.70.00.   1 Platoon at G.18.c.50.30.
1 Platoon at G.18.b.45.20   1 Platoon at G.24.a.20.65.

WAR DIARY
or
INTELLIGENCE SUMMARY.
(Erase heading not required.)

Army Form C. 2118.

Reference Sheet 57c N.W. Edition 9a Local 1/20,000

Place: Trenches

Summary of Events and Information

"B" Company 2 Platoons in Sunken Road from G.18.s.40.25 to G.18.s.80.07.
1 Platoon at G.17.d.35.20.   1 Platoon at G.23.b.20.90.
"D" Company. 1 Platoon at G.18.b.05.25   1 Platoon at G.18.a.80.40.
1 Platoon at G.18.a.50.50.
2 Platoons in Sunken Road - G.18.c.60.98 to G.18.c.60.80.
"C" Company in Trench G.17.c.85.20 to G.23.b.10.90.
Battalion Headquarters G.23.b.30.60.
Casualties ?

August 25th.
Battalion pushed forward in direction of SAPIGNIES - BAPAUME ROAD.
"B" Company Right Front.   "A" Company Left Front.
"C" Company Right Support.   "D" Company Left Support.
The general line from H.14.c.10.75 to H.15.b.70.40 was reached.
Very heavy shelling and intense gas shelling combined with heavy mist apparently disorganised the troops, and the general direction of the attack was lost.
"C" Company remained in the Trench from H.15.c.85.50 to H.13.c.60.70.
"A" Company came back to Trench at H.15.c.40.90.
"B" Company to the Road, G.18.c.60.80 to G.18.a.60.10.
"D" Company to their original position.
As soon as the mist was clear, a reconnaissance was made of the area - SAPIGNIES - BAPAUME Road, and about 10.30 a.m. Battalion pushed forward.
"C" Company occupying Road from H.13.a.05.20 to H.14.b.95.60.
"A" Company H.14.b.95.60 to H.14.b.85.80.
"B" Company H.14.b.50.70 to H.14.b.20.95.
"D" Company in Embankment H.14.d.20.50 to H.14.d.10.70.
6.30 p.m. Battalion moved forward in a Easterly direction in support to 111th Brigade, and established themselves in the vicinity of the SAPIGNIES-BAPAUME Road.

August 26th.
Battalion relieved by K.O.S.B., 5th Division, and withdrew to Huts N.E. of ACHIET-LE-PETIT.

WAR DIARY
or
INTELLIGENCE SUMMARY.
(Erase heading not required.)

Army Form C.2118.

Instructions regarding War Diaries and Intelligence Summaries are contained in F. S. Regs., Part II. and the Staff Manual respectively. Title pages will be prepared in manuscript.

Place	Date	Hour	Summary of Events and Information	Remarks and references to Appendices
Trenches	27/8/18		Battalion in outpost Hutts NE of ACHIET LE PETIT. clearing up and bathing. Casualties 2.O.R.	P.W.A. 2 W.A.
	28/8/18		Battalion Resting. Casualties & Reinforcements NIL.	P.W.A.
	29/8/18		do. SS135 Personnel Regained from ORVILLE. Reinforcements 2.O.R. Casualties NIL. Convicts by R. of L. Band	P.W.A. P.W.A.
	30/8/18		Battalion resting. Events by R. of L. Band Casualties and Reinforcements NIL.	P.W.A. 2 W.A.
	31/8/18		Training carried out. Reinforcements 2/Lieut. WEBBER 2/Lieut. DASHFIELD, 2/Lieut. RUSSELL and 66 O.Rs. Casualties NIL.	2 W.A. P.W.A. P.W.A.

31/8/18.

A. Welch. Lieut. Col.
Comdg 8 Lincolnshire Regt.

63rd Brigade.
37th Division.

8th BATTALION

THE LINCOLNSHIRE REGIMENT.

SEPTEMBER 1 9 1 8

37/63

8 Lincoln Rgt

Army Form C. 2118.

WAR DIARY
or
INTELLIGENCE SUMMARY.
(Erase heading not required.)

98 36

Place	Date	Hour	Summary of Events and Information	Remarks and references to Appendices
ACHIET-LE-PETIT.	1/9/18		Bn resting. Concert by Regt Band. Casualties: Reinforcements Nil.	Nil
do.	2/9/18		do. do. do. do. do.	
TRENCHES.	3/9/18		Bn left ACHIET-LE-PETIT and marched to area just E. of BEUGNY. Casualties Nil.	Sheet 57.C.N.W. do.
do.	4/9/18		Bn relieved 4th MIDDLESEX in camp in I.23.d. + I.30.a. Nth. move forward to I.30.c + d. Casualties Nil.	
do.	5/9/18		Bn: relieved 1st Herts Regt on N.W. Edge of HAVRINCOURT WOOD. Bn H.Q. J.36.c.10.40. A. Coy. R. front. C. Coy. L. front. B. Coy. R. support. D. Coy. L. support. Casualties Nil.	57.C. NE+S.E.
do.	6/9/18		Bn: in trenches. Casualties 1. O.R. Killed. 3. Wounded 3. Gassed.	do.
do.	7/9/18		A. Coy pushed forward to SHROPSHIRE RESERVE. C. Coy found line of post from junction of HENLY LANE & CHEETHAM SWITCH to junction HUBERT AV. & SHROPSHIRE RESERVE. Bn. A.A.R. runs up to W. Edge of Wood at K.36.d. 40.30. Casualties 4. O.R. Wounded 1 Gassed. Heavy shelling with burry Gas etc.	do.
do.	8/9/18		C. Coy pushed forward to CHEETHAM SWITCH. Casualties 2. O.R. Killed 4 Wounded.	do.

Army Form C. 2118.

WAR DIARY
or
INTELLIGENCE SUMMARY.
(Erase heading not required.)

Instructions regarding War Diaries and Intelligence Summaries are contained in F.S. Regs., Part II. and the Staff Manual respectively. Title pages will be prepared in manuscript.

Place	Date	Hour	Summary of Events and Information	Remarks and references to Appendices
TRENCHES	9/9/18		B.Coy. Relived A.Coy. D.Coy relived 1st ESSEX. 2 Platoons in front W of Canal. 1 Platoon att: C.Coy in YORKSHIRE HEAD. Casualties. 1 O.R. Killed 5 Wounded 9 Gassed.	S'Y.C. N.E. & S.E.
	10/9/18		B.Coy. Push forward E. KNIFE TRENCH. Captured 2 Prisoners 1 M.G. and killing 8 Enemy. C.Coy Capt'n. 1 Prisoner while establishing POST E of YORKSHIRE HEAD P. Enemy shelling in front & left of trenches. Casualties 2/Lt.G. Jones Killed. S/O.R. Killed 9 Wounded. 3 Gassed.	
	11/9/18		C.Coy relieved by 2/4. YORK & LANCASTER Regt. B.Coy by 5" K.O.Y.L.I. Bt withdrew to camp W. of LEBUCQUIERE. in I. 29 central. Casualties 3 Wounded.	
LEBUCQUIERE	12/9/18		Bt. at Rest. Casualties Nil.	
	13/9/18		Bt: Resting and Cleaning up. Concert by Reg: Band.	
	14/9/18		Bt: Lying. " " " "	
	15/9/18		Taube brought down—chess in floored. Casualties 1.O.R. Wounded.	

WAR DIARY or INTELLIGENCE SUMMARY

Army Form C. 2118.

Place	Date	Hour	Summary of Events and Information	Remarks and references to Appendices
LESBOEUFS	16/9/18		Bn: relieved 13th R.B. in trenches J.33. L.+d. J.34. a+c. Bn. H.Q. J.27d. 4.4. (Right Bn); in Div; Main line of resistance. Casualties Nil.	Check 5.4.c. N.E.+S.E.
TRENCHES	17/9/18		Bn; Training. Casualties Nil	
	18/9/18		Eny Counter Attack. Bn: manned line of resistance. Attack broke off at Nr Witchew. Casualties 6 O.R. Wounded	
	19/9/18		Bn; Relieved 1st Essex in Centre Batt sector. B Coy Right Front. D.Coy Left Front C. Support + A. Reserve. Bn H.Q. Q.4.d.60.15. Casualties 2 O.R. Wounded	
	20/9/18		Bn: in the line, heavily shelled in evening. Casualties 3.O.R. Wounded	
	21/9/18		The front line withdrew slightly to allow our heavies to bombard it + Eny front line for 4 hours. After this an Eny front-Coy; endeavoured to push forward to get out of this but with considerable resistance. Bn; was relieved by the 1/16 Manchester Regt. + withdrew to Camp at LESBOEUFS. Casualties 5. O.R. Wounded	
	22/9/18		Bn; marched to Camp in area in + about THILLOY. Capt M.H.G. Coy awarded M.C. Reinforcements 63. O.R.	

Army Form C. 2118.

WAR DIARY
or
INTELLIGENCE SUMMARY.
(Erase heading not required.)

Instructions regarding War Diaries and Intelligence Summaries are contained in F. S. Regs., Part II. and the Staff Manual respectively. Title pages will be prepared in manuscript.

Place	Date	Hour	Summary of Events and Information	Remarks and references to Appendices
THILLOY.	23-9-18		Bn: Resting and cleaning up. Casualties Nil. Concert by band.	
	24-9-18		Bn: Inspected by C.O.. Bn. Band performed for Bn in LE BARQUE THEATRE. Concert by band.	
	25-9-18		Bn. Training. Concert by Reg Band.	
	26-9-18		Bn Training. Bn attd lecture by II Corps Education Officer.	
	27-9-18		Bn Training. Concert by Regt Band. Reinforcements 2/Lt J.L. WOODS.	
	28-9-18		Bn Training. Concert by Reg Band.	
	29-9-18		Church Parade. Reg: Party in afternoon. Reinforcements 24/Lt. F.A. STIMPSON, T.C. AHOP, F. BERRY.	
	30-9-18		Bn. marched to camp at ROYAULCOURT.	

In the Field
30/9/18.

A. T. Fitch Lieut Col
Comdg 6 Lincolnshire Regt

63rd Brigade.
37th Divison.

8th BATTALION

THE LINCOLNSHIRE REGIMENT.

OCTOBER 1918

WAR DIARY
or
INTELLIGENCE SUMMARY.

8 Lincolns Regt

Vol 37

Place	Date	Hour	Summary of Events and Information	Remarks and references to Appendices
	OCTOBER 1918.			SHEET. 57c.S.E.
ROYAULCOURT	1st		Bn. Moved into GOUZEAUCOURT WOOD. Bn. H.Q. Q.34.A.20.95.	
	2nd		Bn: Training. Casualties + Reinforcements Nil.	
	3rd		Bn: Training. Concert by Regt. Band. Reinforcements 2/Lt. O.C.TERRY. Casualties Nil.	
	4th		Bn: Training. Working parties of 3 Coys: under C.R.E. Reinforcements + Casualties Nil.	
	5th		Bn: Training. Concert by Regt. Band. Reinforcements + Casualties Nil.	
	6th		Bn: Moved to area N. of GONNELIEU. Bn. H.Q. in Quarry Out R.21.c.65.00.	
	7th		Bn: Resting. Reinforcements + Casualties Nil.	
TRENCHES.	8th		Bn: Moved to SLATE COPSE. Bn. H.Q. M.22.c.15.40. Bn: Moved to PELU WOOD after	57c.S.W.
			which the Bn: advanced through the 112 Bde (at 17.30) + took up a line	
			R. front line N.16.b.10.80 to N.11.c.30.85. L. front line N.11.c.30.85 to N.11.a.05.45.	
			R. Support Coy. N.10.a.20.45 to N.10.c.40.40. Reserve Coy. N.9.c.95.40 to N.9.b.00.30.	
			Bn. H.Q. N.9.c.65.40.	
			Casualties 8.O.R. Killed + Wounded 24.O.R. 2/Lt. BERRY. F.	
			2/Lt. HALL. J.R. 2/Lt. Gopsie Drax injd.	
			2/Lt. Lewis Fisher injd Staff.	

WAR DIARY
or
INTELLIGENCE SUMMARY.
(Erase heading not required.)

Army Form C. 118.

Place	Date	Hour	Summary of Events and Information	Remarks and references to Appendices
	OCTOBER 9th.		At 0530 the Bn: Advanced to a line R.T.L Coy: 2 Platoons O.I.C.60.10 & O.I.C.40.40 & Platoons O.I.C.40.00. to O.I.C.20.30. Left Front Coy. O.I.A.20.00 to O.I.A.00.55. 2 Platoons N.6.b. 90.00. to N.6.b. 95.50. Right Support. N.12.C.15.85. to N.12.a.50.15. 2 Platoons N.6.C.70.00. to N.6.C.20.25. Left Support Coy: 2 Platoons N.5.C.90.90 to N.5.D.10.20. 2 Platoons. N.10.b. 90.80 to N.11.a. 10.30. Bn.H.Q. Moved to HARCOURT. at 1700 Bn. H.Q. Moved to HARCOURT. Casualties Lt. A.B. WIGGINS. Wounded 1.O.R. Wounded.	Sheet 57/3. S.W.
	10th		Bn. Moved via :— HAVCOURT, LIGNY, & CAVORY to area around AVDENCOURT. Afterwards advancing through the 112 Bde taking up a line from D. 30.d. 20.30 - J.6.d. 65.40. Two Companies distributed in depth. R. Support Coy. J.11.d.30.00 to J.11.d. 40.60. Left Support Coy. J.10.b. 50.15 to J.10.B. 80.25. Bn: H.Q. J.16.d. 30.80. During this advance the Btn was heavily shelled. Casualties Killed 3.O.R. Wounded. 34.O.R. + 2Lt. RUSSELL. J.C.	SHEET. 57/B. NE.
	11th		An Officer & 1 Platoon of L. Front. Coy. advanced across the RIVER. SELLE established themselves at E.25.a. 20.00 to E.25.C. 30.95.	

H. Gordon Deans Major
E.W. Lancashire Regt

WAR DIARY
or
INTELLIGENCE SUMMARY.
(Erase heading not required.)

Army Form C. 118.

Place	Date	Hour	Summary of Events and Information	Remarks and references to Appendices
	OCTOBER			
	11.	5.	A patrol of the R. Fus. Coy. advanced across the River and took up a position. K.I.a.60.40. Remainder of front line withdrew to Road J.6.b. 60.95: The forward positions were heavily shelled. Casualties. Wounded 13. O.R.	
	12.	5.	2/Lt Te.R.R.Y, O.C. 2/Lt BINKEY. J. Rev. Capt. T.B. HARDY. V.C, D.S.O, M.C. & Bn: Middlesex Regt: to attack the H. Bn: Middlesex Regt: to attack high ground E of the river. Enemy counter attack in evening. Bt: formed line of resistance of 2 Coys. from N.6.C. 30.60 & J.12.A.50.40. Bt. Withdrew to Billets & CAUDRY. Bt.H.Q CAUDRY. Bt. H.Q No 14. Rue de l'Industrie. Casualties. 1.O.R. Wounded.	
CAUDRY.	13.		Bt. Resting. Cleaning up. Concerts by Regimental Band.	
	14.		" Cinema & Concert in Y.M.C.A.	
	15.		" Battalion starting in CAUDRY. Tactical Training carried out.	
	16.		" " "	
	17.		" " "	
	18.		" " " Inspected by G.O.C. Division. Good turn out.	

T.A.Gordon Dean Major
" MAJOR B Henrymr...
H.G. DEAN DSO 3/4 Batallion

WAR DIARY or INTELLIGENCE SUMMARY

Army Form C. 2118.

Place	Date	Hour	Summary of Events and Information	Remarks and references to Appendices
CAUDRY	19/10/18		Battalion resting. Training carried out. Reinforcements 5 Officers & 141 O.R. J.A. WALKER, C. FOX, W.S. HYDE, A.E. BROUGHTON, H.T. WOODLANDS	
	20/10/18		Battalion attended Church Parade in "Sam Browns" Theatre. Final Div Football Competition. Result: 13 KRRC 3 goals, 8th Lincolns 2 goals. 3 Casualties to Transport personnel.	
	21/10/18		Training carried out. LIEUT. W.H. MARTIN MRC USA joined Battalion. Capt T.G.T. Thomas proceeded to 49th Field Ambulance. REV. CHEESE C.F. joined Battalion. Memorial Service for REV. T.B. HARDY V.C. D.S.O. M.C.	
	22/10/18		Training carried out. Battalion moved to BRIASTRE into Divisional Reserve.	
BRIASTRE	23/10/18		" " " BEAURAIN in morning and to arrive	
BEAURAIN	24/10/18		W of NEUVILLE late in the day in X.25.a. Battn HQ at X.25.d 15.95.	
NEUVILLE			Same enemy Bn relieved 1/12th Herts (Left Support Bn). A Coy: 3 Platoons on railway X.22.d 20.65 to X.16 central. Coy HQ X.21.c 90.80.	
			B Coy: 3 Platoons X.21.a 60.80 to X.21.a 50.45. Coy HQ X.21.a 60.50.	
			Posts X.21.a 40.60 to X.21.a 60.40 - Coy HQ X.20.a 60.80.	
			C Coy: Billets in SPEECHES X.20.a 40.00	
			D " " " " X.20.c 60.95. Bn HQ X.20.a 15.30	

WAR DIARY
or
INTELLIGENCE SUMMARY.
(Erase heading not required.)

Army Form C.2118.

Instructions regarding War Diaries and Intelligence Summaries are contained in F.S. Regs., Part II. and the Staff Manual respectively. Title pages will be prepared in manuscript.

Place	Date	Hour	Summary of Events and Information	Remarks and references to Appendices
	25/10/18		'D' Coy relieved 'C' Coy S.L.I. 3 Platoons in Railway X27 a 85-75 to X21 d 5-0-70. 1 Platoon in cellar X26 d 80.90. Coy HQ X27 a 00.70. 'B' Coy relieved 'D' Coy S.L.I. 1½ platoons in Railway from X21 d 70.10 to X22 a 05-60. 1 Platoon in posts at X15-£ 70.40, X15-£ 60.30, X15 d 65-30, X15 d 80.00, 1 Platoon X20a 60.20 to X15 c 60.00. Coy HQ & ½ Platoon X21 £ 60.10. Reserve Platoon 'H' Coy moved to X15 £ 30.00. 'C' Coy altered dispositions 2 Platoons X21a 50.45 to X21a 35-30. 2 Platoons X21 a 60.80 to X21a 5.0.45. Casualties 6 O.R. wounded	
	26/10/18		Bn in same position. Railway heavily shelled with H.E. & Gas. L.G. & Musketry training carried out. 'B' Coy Battle.	
	27/10/18		Bn in same position - 'C' & 'D' Coys Battle. Same evening Bn relieved 1/1st HERTS Rt Front Bn in the line. H/Coy left front Coy - 2 Platoons in Posts X4 £ 78.70 to X5-£ 30.50. 1 Platoon X4 £ 60.00 - X5 c 00.78 1 Platoon in cellar X4 d 35-36. Coy H.Q. X4 d 65-35. 'B' Coy Left Front Coy - 2½ Platoons in 7 posts X5 c 35.40 to X11a 60.70. ½ Platoon in road X11a 45.65 to X11a 40.70. 1 Platoon & Coy H.Q. X5 c 00.15. 'C' Coy Left support Coy in cellar X4 d 55-35 to X4 d 30.40. Coy HQ X4 d 78.18. 'D' Coy Right Support Coy - 2 Platoons in Railway X11a 35-28 to X11c 05.60. 1 Platoon in Posts X11 a 05.25 & X11a 15.20. 1 Platoon in cellar X4 d 72.20 Coy HQ cellar X5 c 10.15. Battalion Hqs X4 d 55-30 Casualties 1 O.R. wounded	
	28/10/18		Battalion in the line. Heavy shelling in the early morning. Casualties 7 O.R. wounded	
	29/10/18		Battalion in the line. Casualties 1 O.R. killed 2 O.R. wounded 2/Lt BRUMBER wounded	
	30/9/18		In the line. Shelled heavily. Casualties 2 O.R. wounded	
	31/10/18		In the line. Casualties 2 O.R. wounded	

H Gordon Major
2/Lieutenant A/Adjt
8.

63rd Brigade.
37th Division.

8th BATTALION

THE LINCOLNSHIRE REGIMENT.

NOVEMBER 1918

8th Lincolnshire Regt.

Vol 38

Army Form C 2118.

WAR DIARY or INTELLIGENCE SUMMARY.

(Erase heading not required.)

Instructions regarding War Diaries and Intelligence Summaries are contained in F. S. Regs., Part II. and the Staff Manual respectively. Title pages will be prepared in manuscript.

Place	Date	Hour	Summary of Events and Information	Remarks and references to Appendices
	NOVEMBER			
	1/11/18		Battn in the Line. — Sheet 57ᴬ S.E. "C" Coy relieved "D" Coy 2ⁿᵈ LINCOLN Regt. 1 Platoon posts at X.11.d.20-30 & X.17.b.35-95 — 1 platoon posts X.11.d.30-65 — X.11.Z.12.05 — 1 platoon X.10.70.45 & X.11.d.85-00 — 1 platoon X.11.c.90-50 to X.11.c.95-15 — Coy HQ. X.11.c.96-10. "B" Coy relieved to GHISSIGNIES. Left front platoon relieved by 2ⁿᵈ MIDDLESEX Regt & Right front platoon by our "B" Coy. Disposition — 1 Platoon X.4.d.60.00 to X.5.c.00-78 — 1 Platoon in cellar X.5.a.35-65. 2 Platoons in cellars X.4.d.55-35 & X.4.d.30-40. "B" Coy (Left front Coy) held line posts from X.5.c.30-50 to X.11.a.60.70. "D" Coy moved 1 platoon in cellar at X.4.d.72.20 to cellar at X.5.c.05-15. Casualties 1 O.R. wounded.	
	2/11/18		In the Line. — "B" Coy raided posts at Lieut Cooney on X.5.a. at 23.45 hrs. Between 30 & 40 casualties inflicted on enemy. Heavy resistance offered. Casualties 11 O.R. killed 13 O.R. wounded 10 R. missing 1 O.R. wounded.	
	3/11/18		In the Line — Found Mortar activity in front Line — Casualties 12 O.R. killed 17 O.R. wounded. 1 O.R. missing, 1 wounded acc. shrapnel wound.	
	4/11/18		Bn relieved by 111 Inf Bgde — "A" Coy withdrew to cellars in GHISSIGNIES — Coy HQ X.4.d.20.30 "B" Coy withdrew to cellars X.5.c.00.15 & X.5.c.15-70 "C" Coy withdrew to SALECHES in area X.19.d. "D" Coy withdrew 2 platoons to SOLECHES in X.19.d. — 2 platoons relieved Left Flank 111 Inf Bgde outposts at the evening 2 orchards in vicinity of Chapel on X.5.a.2.6 & X.5.c.2.0.1. — 1 platoon established posts X.5.c.30.55 to R.5.c.0.15.15. 1 platoon X.5.a.20-70 to X.5.a.10.90. 24 prisoners captured in this operation. Workers from the South 2 platoons of B.Coy outflanked Railway to Lieut Cooney on X.5.a. "C" Coy & 2 platoons of "D" Coy on SALECHES moved forward to GHISSIGNIES. Excellent in cellars. The two front platoons of D Coy were also withdrawn to GHISSIGNIES. In the evening the Bn moved to LOUVIGNY in area S.8 & 9 L. Br HQ S.7.d.3.0.66. The Bn established same areas in GHISSIGNIES resting for the night in cellars. Bn HQ X.5.c.2.0.25. Casualties 5 O.R. killed 8 O.R. wounded. 2 O.R. Missing. 2 Lt BEAGLES killed. 2 Lt HYDE & 2 Lt FOX wounded.	

A.W. Mitchell Lt Col |

WAR DIARY or INTELLIGENCE SUMMARY.

Army Form C. 2118

Instructions regarding War Diaries and Intelligence Summaries are contained in F. S. Regs., Part II. and the Staff Manual respectively. Title pages will be prepared in manuscript.

(Erase heading not required.)

Place	Date	Hour	Summary of Events and Information	Remarks and references to Appendices
NEVILLE	5-11-16		7th Batt moved back to NEVILLE. Reinforcements + Casualties Nil	
	6-11-16		Batt resting. Coy battle Reinforcements + Casualties Nil	
	7-11-16		Batt training. Reinforcements 41 O.R. Casualties Nil	
	8-11-16		Batt training. Reinforcements 29 O.R. Casualties Nil	
	9-11-16		Batt training. Reinforcements + Casualties Nil	
	10-11-16		Church Parade. Reinforcements + Casualties Nil	
	11-11-16		Batt moved to Cavalry. Reinforcements + Casualties Nil	57 B/400000
CAVALRY	12-11-16		Batt cleaning up. Reinforcement + Casualties Nil	
	13-11-16		Batt training. Reinforcement + Casualties Nil	
	14-11-16		Batt training. Reinforcement + Casualties Nil	
	15-11-16		Batt training. Battn Inspection. Reinforcement + Casualties Nil	
	16-11-16		Batt training. "A" Coy battle Reinforcement 6 O.R. Casualties Nil	
	17-11-16		Church Parade. Reinforcements + Casualties Nil	
	18-11-16		Batt training. Reinforcements + Casualties Nil	
	19-11-16		Batt training. Bn Commanders Inspection "D" Coy battle Reinforcement 1 O.R. Casualties Nil	
	20-11-16		Batt training. H.Q. battle Reinforcements + Casualties Nil	
	21-11-16		Batt training. "A" Coy battle Reinforcements + Casualties Nil	
	22-11-16		Divisional inspection + march past by G.O.C. Division Reinforcements at Horseshoe 2. Casualties Nil	
	23-11-16		Batt training. Reinforcements at Peronne F.T. Casualties Nil	
	24-11-16		Church Parade. "C" Coy battle Reinforcement 2/Lt Mayfort T. + 2/Lt Scamp J Cas Nil	
	25-11-16		Batt training. "D" Coy battle Reinforcement 126 O.R. Casualties Nil	
	26-11-16		Batt training. Lecture by P.O. Athins. Reinforcement Capt Romanoff W.g. Cas Nil	
	27-11-16		Batt training. Bayonet Route March "A" Coy battle Reinforcement + Casualties Nil	
	28-11-16		Batt training. "B" Coy battle Reinforcement 2/Lt Jenney J. + 5 O.R. Cas Nil	
	29-11-16		Batt training. "C" Coy battle Reinforcements 2 O.R. Casualties Nil	
	30-11-16		Batt training. "D" Coy battle Reinforcements + Casualties Nil	

A.C.Tothill Lt Col

63rd Brigade.
37th Division.

8th BATTALION

THE LINCOLNSHIRE REGIMENT

DECEMBER 1918

Army Form C. 2118.

WAR DIARY
or
INTELLIGENCE SUMMARY.
(Erase heading not required.)

Place	Date	Hour	Summary of Events and Information	Remarks and references to Appendices
CAUDRY.	1.12.18		Bn: Moved to MONTRECOURT.	
MONTRECOURT	2.12.18		Bn: Moved to VILLERS Pol.	
VILLERS Pol.	3.12.18		Bn: Cleaning up and resting. Bn: ambushed on the main VALENCIENNES – LE QUESNOY road to receive the passing of His Majesty the King.	
"	4.12.18		Bn: Training. Inspection of Billets by C.O. Reinforcements 4. O.R.	
"	5.12.18		Bn: Training. Bn: recreation room opened.	
"	6.12.18		Bn: Training. Reinforcements 23. O.R. Concert by Regt. Band.	
"	7.12.18		Bn: Training. Rugby football match Off: of 63rd v. 4th Bn N. H⁹ F.A. drawn.	
"	8.12.18		Bn: Church Parade. Inspection of billets by C.O. Reinforcements Y. O.R.	
"	9.12.18		Bn: Training. Lecture Match Off: v. Sergts. Result. Light 3. Off: 1. Lectr. by Rev. W.F. Klich on The British Manual Ruling. Fin July to Dec 14-14. Reinforcements 3. O.R.	
"	10.12.18		Bn: Training. Rugby Practice Match. Reinforcements 2. O.R.	
"	11.12.18		Bn: Training. Rugby football match Off: of 63rd Bde v. 1st Norfolks at Le Quesnoy. Result drawn. Reinforcements 2. O.R.	
"	12.12.18		Bn: Training. B. Coy Buttles Concert by Regt Band.	
"	13.12.18		Bn: Training. Concert by Henry Smith in evening. C. Coy Battled.	
"	14.12.18		Bn: Moved to BAVAI. Bn: The Concert by Coathall.	
BAVAI.	15.12.18		Bn: Moved to BOIS-LE-BOIS.	
SOUS-LE-BOIS	16.12.18		Bn: Resting. Lecture at Inspection of Billets by C.O. Concert by Regt Band.	A.V. Fitch Lt Col

Army Form C. 2118.

WAR DIARY
or
INTELLIGENCE SUMMARY.
(Erase heading not required.)

Instructions regarding War Diaries and Intelligence Summaries are contained in F. S. Regs., Part II. and the Staff Manual respectively. Title pages will be prepared in manuscript.

Place	Date	Hour	Summary of Events and Information	Remarks and references to Appendices
SOUS-LE-BOIS	17.12.18		Bk: Moved to GRAND RENG.	
GRAND-RENG	18.12.18		Bk: Moved to BINCHE.	
BINCHE	19.12.18		Bk: Moved to COURCELLES.	
COURCELLES	20.12.18		Bk: Moved to FRASNES-LEZ-GOSSELIES.	
FRASNES-LEZ-GOSSELIES	21.12.18		Bk: Resting and cleaning up.	
"	22.12.18		Bk: C. of E. Parade. Concert by Reg Band.	
"	23.12.18		Bk: Training.	
"	24.12.18		Bk: Training.	
"	25.12.18		Church Parade. Xmas dinners for men by companies. Bk: Officers dinner at 2.30 P.M. Concert by Band at 11 A.M.	
"			Bk: Concert at 6 P.M.	
"	26.12.18		Football Match. Off v Sergt. Result. Off 1, Sergt 1.	
"	27.12.18		Bk Training. Football match B. Coy v. remainder of Bk. Result. B. Coy 3. Rest of Bk 0. Rupfrick. 6. O.R.	
"	28.12.18		Bk Training. B Coy Bathed. Concert by Reg Band.	
"	29.12.18		C. of E. Church Parade. Concert by Reg Band.	
"	30.12.18		Bk. Training. Bk. Football Match (New Reg—) Bk. V. 123 Bde R.F.A. Result. Bk. 3. R.F.A. 0.	
"	31.12.18		Bk Training. Bk. Drill. Lecture by Capt. F. A. Allhuser "Remobilization".	

A. I. Hitch Lt. Col
& A. Turcotur

Army Form C. 2118.

WAR DIARY
or
INTELLIGENCE SUMMARY.
(Erase heading not required.)

Instructions regarding War Diaries and Intelligence Summaries are contained in F.S. Regs., Part II. and the Staff Manual respectively. Title pages will be prepared in manuscript.

8 Lincoln

Place	Date	Hour	Summary of Events and Information	Remarks and references to Appendices
FRASNES LEZ GOSSELIES.	JAN. 1919.			
	1		Bn. Training. Concert by B. Coy in evening.	
	2		Bn. Training. Bn. Recreation Room opened at Cantin in Village.	
	3		Bn. Training. Bn. played 1st Bn: League Soccer Match V. 10th Royal Fusiliers at JUMET. Result: Lincolns 2. R.F. 1.	
	4		Bn. Training. Honours and Awards. M.C. 2nd Lt. F.A. Stephen. 2nd Lt. C. Fox. D.C.M. Sergt. G. White. M.M. Bent H. Robinson. Concert by Winney links in evening including Sketch by H.Q. Officers. Cheque for £100 rec'd for Band fund from 2nd A. Black. Bank: Grimsby	
	5		Bn: Church Parade. Inter-Coy: football in afternoon.	
	6		Bn: Training. Bn. Drill. Honours & Awards. Mentioned in dispatches. T/Capt. W. Horn. D.S.O.	
			T/Capt. G.P. Jones.	
	7		Bn. Training. Reinforcements. Capt: S.L. Bromfield. M.C. Bn. played 2nd Bn: League Soccer Match V. 1/1st Herts Regt. on our own ground. Result Herts 3. Lincolns 1.	
	8		Bn: Training. Reinforcement 13. O.R.	
	9		Bn. Training. Honours and Awards. Bar to M.C. 2nd Lt. E.P. Welby M.C.	
	10		Bn. Training. Reinforcements Capt A.G. Hoyte M.C. Bn: Played 1st Div. League Match V. D.A.C. & their ground. Result Lincolns 1. D.A.C. 2.	
	11		Bn: Training. Bn: Drill. Reinforcement. 6.O.R.	

A. Hitch Lieut-Colonel
Cdg. 8th Bn. Lincolnshire Regt.

Army Form C. 2118.

WAR DIARY
or
INTELLIGENCE SUMMARY.
(Erase heading not required.)

Place	Date	Hour	Summary of Events and Information	Remarks and references to Appendices
FRASNES LEZ GOSELIES	JAN. 1919 12.		Bn.: Church Parade. Reinforcements 1.O.R. Inter Coy football.	
	13		Bn.: Training. Lecture by M.O.	
	14		Bn.: Training. Court of Enquiry. Missing kits, including M. Cle. Kent-i-Oven.	
	15		Bn.: Training. Reinforcements 1.O.R. Bn.: Played Rom League Match V. R.A.S.C. (Air Force) Signor Vitaline + M. Morrie.	
			Reinft. Linds 6 R.A.P.C. 1.	
	16.		Bn.: Training.	
	17.		Bn.: Training. Bn. Drill.	
	18		Bn.: Training. Court by Missing kits. Reinforcements 4. O.R.	
	19.		Bn.: Church Parade. Bn. Played Rom League Match. V. R.A.M.C. on own ground.	
			Reinft. R.A.M.C. 2. Lincolns. 1.	
	20.		Bn.: Training.	
	21.		Bn.: Training. Lecture by Lt. Col. Alpin. D.P.C. Reconstruction.	
	22		Bn.: Training. Bn.: Played Rom League Match. V. 13th K.R.R.C. Reinft. K.R.R.C. 2. Lincolns 0.	
	23.		Bn.: Training. Bn. Drill. Concert by Missing kits followed by Dance.	
	24.		Bn.: Training.	

A. White
Lieut-Colonel
Cdg. 8th Bn. Lincolnshire Regt.

Army Form C. 2118.

WAR DIARY
or
INTELLIGENCE SUMMARY.
(Erase heading not required.)

Instructions regarding War Diaries and Intelligence Summaries are contained in F. S. Regs., Part II. and the Staff Manual respectively. Title pages will be prepared in manuscript.

Place	Date	Hour	Summary of Events and Information	Remarks and references to Appendices
FRASNES. LEZ. GOSSELIES.	JAN 25.		Bn: Training. Bn. Played Div: League Match V. 4th Middlesex Regt on our own ground. Result 4th Middlesex 1. Lincolns 1. Gained by Winning lines followed by draw.	
	26.		Bn: Church Parade.	
	27.		Bn: Training. Lecture by Lt. A.M. Anderson. "Napoleon & the Lened Rev".	
	28.		Bn: Training. Honours and Awards. Meritorious Service Medal. R.Q.M.S. Mell. C.Q.M.S. Southgate.	9.
	29.		Bn: Training. Lecture by Capt: Grant on Rhodesia.	
	30.		Bn: Training. Dance in Convent Hall.	
	31.		Bn: Training.	

A. Ritch,
Lieut-Colonel
Cdg. 8th Bn. Lincolnshire Regt.

WAR DIARY or INTELLIGENCE SUMMARY.

Army Form C. 2118.

(Erase heading not required.)

Instructions regarding War Diaries and Intelligence Summaries are contained in F.S. Regs., Part II. and the Staff Manual respectively. Title pages will be prepared in manuscript.

Place	Date	Hour	Summary of Events and Information	Remarks and references to Appendices
FRASNES LEZ GOSSELIES	FEB: 1919			
	1		Bn: Training. Whist Drive in Bn: Recreation Room.	
	2		Brigade Parade to rehearse for Colour presentation.	
	3		Bn: Training. Presentation of ~~Colours~~ Colours to Bn: by the Corps Commander Lt: Gen: Sir G.H. Harper. K.C.B. D.S.O. Escort of Massey Shiel on every.	
	4		Bn: Training. Bn: Route March.	
	5		Bn: Training. Lecture by H: Comm: General. on "The Work of the Mayor."	
	6		Bn: Training. Lecture by "Riflemen Dillon. English as She is Spoke."	
	7		Bn: Training. Lecture by Rev: E.D. Martin "The League of Nations". Bn: found supply dump Guard at MONTIGNY. 250. Other ranks under command of Capt: A.O. Garvey.	
	8		Bn: Training	
	9		Voluntary Church Services. C.O.'s Conference	
	10		Bn: Training. Presentation of Medal Ribands by Div: Commander to recipients 63 Bde.	G.
	11		Bn: Training. Lecture by Brig: Gen Ashfield on "The Maley Peninsular."	P.

Alewale
Lieut-Colonel
Cdg. 8th Bn Lincolnshire Regt

Army Form C. 2118.

WAR DIARY
or
INTELLIGENCE SUMMARY.
(Erase heading not required.)

Place	Date	Hour	Summary of Events and Information	Remarks and references to Appendices
FRASNES LEZ GOSSELIES.	FEB: 1919.			
	12.		Bn: Training.	
	13.		Bn: Training. Lecture by Div: Commander, on "Waterloo."	
	14.		Bn: Training.	
	15.		Bn: Training. Honours and Award. Decoration: Militaire (Belgian) Pte. G. Spencer. D.Coy.	
	16.		Church Parade. Inspection of Billets by Bricd in Command.	
	17.		Amalgamation of Companies. A + B. Coys. to form No.1. Coy. C + D. Coys. to form No.2. Coy.	
	18.		No.1.Coy under command of Capt M.G. Rowcroft. No.2.Coy. Capt. H.A.G. autrey. Wind Ends "Performed at Gosselies in "Div Concert Competition."	
	18.		Bn Training. "Musing Ends" Performed at G. anilies as yesterday.	
	19.		Bn: Training.	
	20.		Bn: Training.	
	21.		Bn: Training.	
	22.		Bn: Training. Concert - by "Musing Ends" followed by "Ball."	
	23.		Church Parade.	

Lieut-Colonel
1/5th Bn. Lincolnshire Regt.

Army Form C. 2118.

WAR DIARY
or
INTELLIGENCE SUMMARY.
(Erase heading not required.)

Instructions regarding War Diaries and Intelligence Summaries are contained in F. S. Regs., Part II. and the Staff Manual respectively. Title pages will be prepared in manuscript.

Place	Date	Summary of Events and Information	Remarks and references to Appendices
	FEB. 1919		
FRASNES LEI.	24.	Bn: Training.	
	25.	Bn: Training.	
GOSSELIES	26.	Bn: Training. All Public Places of entertainment out of Bounds.	
	27.	Bn: Training.	
	28.	Bn: Training. Bn. Route March. 1st elop of Bri: Race Meeting at GOSSELIES.	

O. F. Fitch
Lieut-Colonel
O/dg. 8th Bn. Lincolnshire Regt.

8 Lincolns Regt
Army Form C. 2118.

WAR DIARY
or
INTELLIGENCE SUMMARY.
(Erase heading not required.)

Instructions regarding War Diaries and Intelligence Summaries are contained in F. S. Regs., Part II. and the Staff Manual respectively. Title pages will be prepared in manuscript.

Place	Date	Hour	Summary of Events and Information	Remarks and references to Appendices
FRASNES-LEZ-GOSSELIES.	MARCH 1919			
	1		Bn: Training.	
	2		Bn: Church Parade. Summer time came into use.	
	3		Bn: Training.	
	4		Bn: Training.	
	5		Bn: Training. Influenza restrictions on all public places removed.	
	6		Bn: Training. Two Coy. sufficient march fete. 1 Off. + 25 O.R. to load shell at MOTTE Station.	
	7		Bn: Training. Working party to MOTTE.	
	8		Bn: Training. Working party to MOTTE. Advance billeting party left for new area.	
	9		Bn: Church Parade till Concert-Room.	
	10		Bn: found supply tram guard at MONTIGNIES. 4 Off. + 40 O.R.	
			Rest of Bn: moved to Jumet area JUMET area. Bn: H.Q. 161 Rue de Jumet Roux.	
JUMET.	11		Training under Coy. Arrangements.	
	12		Bn: Training.	
	13		Bn: Training.	
	14		Bn: Training.	
	15		Bn: Training.	
	16		Bn: Church Parade in Circle de Jumet.	

WAR DIARY
or
INTELLIGENCE SUMMARY.
(Erase heading not required.)

Army Form C. 2118.

Place	Date	Hour	Summary of Events and Information	Remarks and references to Appendices
JUMET.	MARCH 1919. 17.		Bn: Training. Lecture by M.O. on Venereal Disease.	
	18.		Bn: Training. Y.M.C.A. Canteen & Recreation Room Opened at JUMET.	
	19.		Bn: Training.	
	20.		Bn: found special fatigue. 2 proceed to CHARLEROI. 5 th. O.R. & 3 Off. under command of Capt. Gong	
	21.		Bn: Training. Concert by Minny Lewis in "Circe at Jumet"	
	22.		Bn: Training. Concert by Minny Lewis in "Belle de la Caronde, Roux."	
			Draft of 80. O.R. proceeded to the 28th P.of W. Coy. Calais.	
	23.		Bn: Church Parade. Draft of 80. O.R. proceeded to 29th P.W. Coy: Calais.	
	24.		Nos. 1 & 2. Coys Amalgamated.	
	25. 26. 27. 28. 29.		Bn: being reduced to Cadre strength.	
	30.		Capt. Rowcroft, Lt. Tunney & 2 Lt. McBean. proceeded to join 39th P.of W. Coy. CALAIS.	
	31.		Bn: Bathed.	

A.W. Fitch, Lieut-Colonel
Cdg. 8th Bn. Lincolnshire Regt.